JOHN TAYLOR

Christianity and Politics
in Africa

GREENWOOD PRESS, PUBLISHERS
WESTPORT, CONNECTICUT

Library of Congress Cataloging in Publication Data

Taylor, John Vernon, 1914-
    Christianity and politics in Africa.

    Reprint of the 1957 ed. published by Penguin
Books, London, which was issued as WA9 of Penguin
African series.
    Bibligraphy: p.
    1. Christianity and politics. 2. Africa--
Politics and government--1960-   I. Title.
BR115.P7T29 1979   261.7   79-32
ISBN 0-8371-5951-2

First published in 1957 by Penguin Books, Ltd.,
Harmondsworth, Middlesex, England

Reprinted with the permission of Penguin Books, Ltd.

Reprinted in 1979 by Greenwood Press, Inc.
51 Riverside Avenue, Westport, CT 06880

Printed in the United States of America

10 9 8 7 6 5 4 3 2 1

CONTENTS

PREFACE

WHILE I alone can be called to account for all the opinions expressed in this book, it is not just an individual essay. Some years ago a request came from Africa to the Christian Frontier Council that it would arrange for some fresh thinking to be done about Christian political responsibility there. In consequence, a small group of men with special knowledge was formed in London. They entered into communication with a large number of Africans and Europeans in various parts of Africa, asking them what were their most pressing political problems and what they considered to be the right Christian approach to them. The many letters and memoranda that were thus received in London were carefully considered and compared. Eventually, on the basis of all these data and of the extensive discussions that had taken place, I was asked to write in my own way a book that would make available to readers in Africa, and indeed wherever people are concerned about the future of Africa, the things that we all felt it was most necessary to say at the present time.

The Christian Frontier Council is a body of Christian lay people of all denominations. It seeks, through books like this and through its periodical, *Christian News-Letter*, to focus attention on social and political questions which ought to be disturbing the Christian conscience. Further information about the Council and its methods can be obtained from the Secretary, Christian Frontier Council, 24 St Leonard's Terrace, London sw3.

J. T.

CHAPTER ONE

Should Christians Take Part in Politics?

TO-DAY it is not possible to live in Africa and to be indifferent to political questions. In the most remote villages there are some who have travelled to the towns or plantations or mines for work and have brought back news of the great changes that are taking place. The most backward tribes are affected by community development plans, and their Chiefs are confronted by new problems of social change. Wherever there is a man who can read, there the newspapers will somehow find their way. Rumours of fear and tensions penetrate along every bus and lorry route; the ferment of change is carried in every basket of goods along the paths linking the market places with the peasant homes.

There is certainly no shortage of news to argue about, for events are racing forward at bewildering speed. On the Niger and the Nile new nations are in the making; from Tangier to Tananarive constitutions are in the melting pot; the mysterious initials of new political associations crop up like mushrooms overnight. From Cape to Cairo people are talking of new laws, new strife, new government commissions; new railways, new harbours, new mineral deposits. The planes which carry traders and technicians from Europe to Africa fly back again with students, members of deputations, and African Commissioners with their staffs.

This situation offers a tremendous challenge to the Church. At a time when men are moving into deep tides of emotion, grappling with complicated problems in the midst of rising tension, and laying out the foundations of future nations, the Church is more than ever needed to proclaim the Word which God is speaking, to demonstrate the way of Christ, and to offer her own embracing fellowship for the healing of the nations. A Church which was strong in faith and wisdom could speak to-day, as she has sometimes spoken in other places and at other times, a prophetic word to make clear the way of justice and tolerance and human dignity. She could hold before men's eyes the values of the spirit, saving them from the false choices of materialism and the false claims of a totalitarian way.

A Church that was true to her calling could exercise a ministry of reconciliation between persons and factions divided by race, creed, or policy, commending by her own example the power of frankness, patience, and negotiation. She could offer the support of her fellowship to all men of goodwill who are bearing the burden of leadership and policy-making. Above all, she could contribute supremely to the building of a people's character: for without that essential material in every race no nation or federation can be firmly built, no matter how right its constitution or its laws may be. Mordecai's words to Esther might truly be spoken to the Church in Africa to-day: 'Who knoweth whether thou art not come to the kingdom for such a time as this?' (Esther 4. 14). But in face of such opportunity the majority of Christians of all races in Africa seem dangerously unprepared for the task.

A Christian, whether he is black or brown or white, recognizes certain fairly clear patterns of duty in his home and neighbourhood and even in his work. He knows he should not get drunk or lose his temper with his family or swindle a fellow man; he accepts an ideal of kindness and honesty and service, even though he may personally fall short of it. But he is not so clearly aware of any Christian pattern of behaviour when he turns to political or social affairs. Has his religion anything to say about the political rights of the different races and tribes in Africa? And, if it has, is it 'practical politics'? Have Christians, as such, had the slightest influence on the formulation of the policies of the Convention People's Party in the Gold Coast or the decisions of the trade unions in Northern Rhodesia? Or is it really true, after all, that as far as such spheres of life are concerned he might just as well not be a Christian for all the difference it makes?

Should Christians Take Part in Politics?

If the Church in Africa (by which is meant the whole Christian community spread throughout Africa, but focused, as it must be, in the congregations of the locally organized Churches) gives the impression that God is not concerned with man's social and political affairs, then men will not be very much concerned with such a God. And this is not because men wish to use God for their own ends and demand that his thoughts shall be their thoughts; but if they feel that God cares nothing for the things which vitally affect their daily lives and stir their deepest emotions, they will not easily be persuaded that such a God loves them in any real sense at all.

In the whole of tropical Africa one in ten of the population is Christian, and there are wide areas in which every single Chief is nominally a Christian. There are many African Christians who have for a long time understood that the God of the Bible is the God of politics also. Yet it remains true that the Church as a whole is not exercising the influence on the changing scene of African affairs which is required of her.

One reason for this is the inadequacy of the Church's leadership. The Church does not consist of her clergy only, and those who use the word 'Church' when they mean the ministry are apt to make the most misleading statements. Yet everywhere it is true that the clergy are the natural spokesmen of the Church's faith, and it is they who mainly guide and administer her life and action; so if the ministry is weak or bewildered, the Church's witness can be neither clear nor strong. Bishop Stephen Neill reported after his survey in East and West Africa in 1950 that in the main the African clergy at that time were 'far from being adequate to the demands that must be made upon them if the Church is to fulfil the role which God seems to be laying upon it in the present time'.[1]

The causes of this weakness are mainly historical. Early missionaries in every part of Africa had to choose between

1. *Survey of the Training of the Ministry in Africa* (International Missionary Council, 1950), Part 1, p. 10.

9

two schools of thought regarding the standards to be required of an African ministry. Some, notably the Roman Catholics, took the view that the indigenous clergy must have qualifications comparable to their European colleagues; and in some parts of Africa this has meant a predominantly foreign ministry supplemented by a small number of highly trained Africans.

But a majority of Missions adopted the other view, that the ministry should be mainly indigenous from the earliest time possible. The Methodists in parts of West Africa have been fortunate in being able to build up a body of qualified African pastors, who have for many years greatly out-numbered European missionaries. Other Missions have accepted men on the grounds of their personal devotion and long experience in the work, rather than their school education, which, at the beginning, was in any case not available. All these Churches drew their ministers from many different walks of life, often from among their own catechists and teachers. Many a man with very little general education (in the first generation of the Church he was sometimes a Chief's son) advanced through alternate periods of training up a kind of 'ladder': first junior and then senior catechist, until at last he was accepted, as a man of middle age, for ordination.

No doubt it was originally hoped that as the general standard of education in the country began to rise, so the qualifications required of the new clergy would be similarly raised. But the inability of the Church to provide salaries comparable to those being offered in government service or commerce was a strong deterrent against the more educated young men who might offer themselves for the ministry. In most areas in tropical Africa there is an ever-widening gulf between the majority of the African clergy and the younger, educated laity in their Churches. At the local district level and in the ordinary councils of the Church, the average priest or pastor may show the ordinary countryman's shrewd wisdom and a more considerable gift of leadership than many observers have given him credit for. But neverthe-less it is generally true that these 'village Hampdens' are baffled by problems of the new world which lie outside their limited experience. And even in those areas where better trained Church leaders do exist,

they are everywhere in short supply and their training is rarely adequate, especially in the special field of relating the universal Gospel to the social and cultural conditions of Africa – an area naturally outside the purview of standard European works on pastoral theology![1]

The seriousness of this weakness in the Church has been intensified by the steady depletion in the ranks of the missionaries since the Second World War – always excepting the Roman Missions – owing to a variety of social and economic factors in Europe. The men who might now be sharing with African colleagues the adventure of tackling the problems of parish work in the new African towns, who might be giving experienced Christian insight into social and economic problems to the pupils in senior secondary schools, or exploring the Christian point of view in discussion groups with the young African intelligentsia: such men are no longer there. And those who remain as missionaries are mostly so tied to the administration of existing institutions that they have no time to develop the new lines of responsible Christian witness which the situation demands.

Of course the Church in Africa could be in a far stronger position if it were willing to muster all its resources. Its leadership and initiative are not limited to the African clergy and the members of the Mission bodies. There are African Christians who are on the staffs of universities, in high administrative posts, in journalism, in law, in the trade unions. There are many thousands of white Christians, some of them keenly active members of their Church; and there is a small number of outstanding Asian Christians scattered throughout East and Central Africa. If all these could be mobilized and inspired with a sense of belonging to one

1. George W. Carpenter, 'The role of Christianity and Islam in contemporary Africa'; essay in *Africa Today*, ed. C. G. Haines (Johns Hopkins Press, Baltimore, 1955), p. 108.

another as fellow members in the Body of Christ, the Church would suffer from no lack of leadership.

But in most parts of Africa there is an utterly inadequate conception of the true place of the laity in the Church. This is partly due to the growth of the Church out of the old relationship of the missionary to his flock. He was the father of the Christian household, the teacher of truth and the dispenser of benefits, the head of the station and the real leader of the local Church. He, for his part, was directed and maintained from the central office of his Mission, either by a bishop or by the secretary of his local Mission board. Every activity of the Mission was regulated from that central office and recorded in its files. It was a natural and necessary discipline; but in the course of time the pattern was projected upon the Church which grew out of the Mission.

The African clergy are the functional counterparts of the missionaries whom they succeeded, and like them are expected to be the sole source of the Church's initiative. For the most part African laymen are far too reluctant to take responsibility for action in the Church, while the clergy on their side are often jealous of their position and slow to welcome lay co-operation except under their own restrictive supervision. There are some happy exceptions to this rule, but they are still too rare. Moreover, in many places the African Church tends to think of itself as something self-contained and institutional, as the parent Mission was bound to be. Only that which is on the files in the central office is recognized as part of the Church; only those activities which are initiated and supported from that office are regarded as the Church's work. So it is not easy for a Christian African girl working as a government welfare officer, or a Christian doctor in a government hospital, or a white woman in an independent social settlement in an African township, to feel that they also are fellow workers in a single Christian enterprise, embraced by, and included in, the outgoing love of the one Church.

The people of Europe have for many centuries been familiar with the sight of Christians launching and organizing all kinds of philanthropic and social action, acting independently of the Church as an institution, and sometimes even in opposition to the leaders of the Church. Men and women of faith have founded orphanages and almshouses, started day schools for poor children, worked for prison reform, financed overseas missionaries and formed co-operative societies, in the name of Christ, without waiting for a minute to be passed by a synod or for a committee to be set up by the annual conference.

But that tradition of free-lance Christian action has not had time to develop in Africa. True, the Church has everywhere launched a vast programme of education, considerable medical work, and, here and there, other projects of social welfare. But all these undertakings have been strictly organized and controlled by the central committees of the Church. A too rigid organization on the one hand, and the economics of African society on the other, have largely prevented the appearance of any honorary lay Christian action. Even such movements as the Scouts and Guides often function exclusively in 'closed' denominational groups.

It might be supposed that the responsibilities of the Christian laity would be better understood through the arrival, in these days, of more missionaries with specialist qualifications, venturing into new fields such as agriculture, technical training, moral welfare, and so on. But under present conditions no missionary, man or woman, is strictly a layman; whatever his job, he is, as it were, under contract to the Church, and in much the same relation to it as the clergy and catechists. The missionaries and the non-missionary Europeans are too widely distinct from one another, at least in the eyes of the African Church, and often in their actual relationships.

There is a good deal to be said for Mission Societies deliberately 'secularizing' many of their missionaries; then some would be, in the full sense, in government service, some attached to industrial or municipal bodies, others directly under Church authority, and others again in some independent venture, such as a Red Cross unit or Y.M.C.A. centre,

13

all bound together by nothing more than their common loyalty to their vocation and their membership of the Society which recruited them. In this way the local Church might more easily catch the vision of the true nature of the Body of Christ, not as an organization with strictly defined spheres of action, but as an organism made up of individuals reaching out into all departments of the life of men, to witness and cleanse and restore.

As long as the Church thinks of itself as an institution, and of its work as limited only to the things that are under its own control, it will find itself being pushed back and back as the Welfare State takes on responsibility for more and more spheres of social action. Instead of penetrating with a unique Christian insight and the redeeming Word of God into all the 'secular' spheres of interest, it will be fighting a losing battle to keep its 'Mission hospitals' and 'Church schools' until nothing is left to it but its responsibility for the 'inner life' of its members and the souls that it seeks to save.

Already there is a growing tendency, in many parts of Africa, for the most devout and loyal elements in the Church to adopt this other-worldly attitude towards the ferment of political argument and aspiration which surrounds them. Often they have been disgusted, not by politics as such, but by the corruption and sensationalism that they have seen. But this reaction has an unfortunate effect on many young African men and women, who have been educated in schools that are closely linked with the Church, and have developed there a strongly established ideal of 'service to my people'. If they seek to give expression to it in social and political action, all too often they are made to feel that their Church, so far from supporting them, looks askance at their activities and questions their good faith.

From what has already been said, it is not hard to understand the process of this estrangement between the institutional Church and the young Christian journalists, co-operatives, and politicians. In the first instance it may arise from the failure of the older clergy and Church members to understand the interests and activities of the young laity. In areas like South Africa, where an increasing number of African priests are of the new graduate type, there is the danger of a definite cleavage between the older, less educated, conservative clergy and the young, educated, and strongly radical priests. The latter, on the grounds of their education, are marked out as leaders in their communities, and the tendency for the graduate priest to set himself up as a parson-politician is very strong. In a few instances such younger men have so far abused their authority as to become regular political speakers at semi-pagan rallies and festivals. Through such activities they have naturally still further alienated the confidence of the older clergy, and driven themselves further into the wilderness.

So the ordinary mistrust of age towards youth, common in every country, is joined to the fear of new and uncomprehended problems. Older Church people in Uganda, for example, may shake their heads over the new social welfare clubs; the government department sponsoring the clubs may be too impatient to consider the suspicions, often well-founded, of the old-fashioned local Christians. But in this clash the ones who suffer are the young girls who, fresh from a Christian school, are posted to the clubs as government welfare workers, only to find the Church hostile to their work and doubtful of their morals. Finding condemnation in the Church instead of fellowship, it is not surprising that some of these girls proceed quickly to provide solid grounds for the suspicions of their fellow Christians. Similarly, in countries where the proscribing of a newspaper or the fining of an editor for sedition is a fairly common occurrence, a young journalist who is genuinely hoping to make a Christian contribution to the vernacular press is apt to feel that the Church, so far from supporting him by its prayers and interest, is morbidly wondering how far he will walk along the narrow, slippery path before he too falls.

It is unfortunately true that those who are most politically aware in Africa to-day are not always the most active in religious observance nor the most orthodox in their beliefs. A number of the political leaders are people who have been disciplined by their Churches for offences of one sort or another; some are openly hostile to the Church; a minority are evidently trouble-makers and men of ill-will. This tends to throw a shadow of suspicion over the genuine Christians who enter the political arena, and makes many of the older Church members shy of expressing any political views at all.

Yet if the Church allows such misgivings to govern its attitude towards politically minded Africans, it is guilty of ignoring the important fact that almost all African political leaders were educated at Christian schools; that a majority of them are still professing Christians; and that the bulk of the members of many of the political parties or associations in all parts of Africa are also members of the Christian Church. Besides this, every major political crisis, of course, sweeps large numbers of the politically shy Church members into full and vocal participation in the nationalist movement, from which they never again withdraw. During the two years of the Kabaka's exile from Buganda, for example, many Christians who had previously been quite unwilling to take any part in the activities of political associations in their country suddenly found themselves caught up in the tide of a new patriotism and devoting themselves not only to a daily study of the news, but to a most active participation in the efforts to secure the Kabaka's return. As a result, far more of the Baganda Christians are politically conscious to-day, and only a minority have abandoned their Christianity in the process.

Nevertheless it remains true that there is a natural conservatism in many of the older African clergy, and in a number of missionaries throughout the continent, which makes them prefer things to stay as they are. The present set-up, with its known pattern of relationships between government and Church and Mission, seems to them to present quite enough problems to be getting on with, and they regard as dangerous impatience any move to rush into new patterns with fresh problems which may prove beyond their capacity to understand and overcome. Moreover, the older generation of African clergy in the British territories still feel strongly the reality of the alliance between the Church and the colonial government. The ideology of the great nineteenth-century missionaries, who saw Christianity, Civilization, and Commerce as the three strands of a single Western blessing, still survives in their minds. They cling to the idea that the main function of a Christian colonial government is philanthropic tutelage and protection, and the colonial education policy is interpreted in terms of this alliance. For such people it is hard to see how the Church can properly be associated with men who are violently critical of the colonial government and are even organizing public opinion to oppose its policies.

In some areas also, there is the same sort of long-standing alliance between the local Church and the Chiefs, so that many of the older clergy have felt that it would be disloyal for Christians to support movements for constitutional reform which would reduce or destroy the power of these Chiefs. An observer from Nyasaland suggests that the fact that the Church has always set itself to show that respect which is due to the Chief as the symbol of law and of tribal continuity, and the fact that the Church has accepted the government policy of indirect rule through the Chiefs, may account in part for the slowness of the Church to take sufficiently into account the power and importance of the Congress as a new political force.

It is only too easy for the Church to find a way out of this dilemma of loyalties by taking the view that life must be kept in strictly separate compartments, so that religious activities are never to be confused with political, social or other 'secular' concerns. Unfortunately this is a way of thinking which particularly commends itself to the representatives of any government. Faced with the problems of governing people of many faiths and of no faith, the State assumes that it must be completely neutralist and secular as far as religion is concerned. A very creditable fear of partiality leads some officials and legislators to speak and enact laws, as far as possible, as though religion did not exist. To such a mind the Churches and all other religious communities are simply 'voluntary bodies'. In return for such impartial toleration, governments, on their side, expect the Churches to leave politics and economics just as strictly alone, and to confine themselves to their own purely spiritual compartments of life. Even the Nazis in Germany and the Communists in Russia have professed to tolerate the Churches on such terms as these.

It is strange to find a somewhat similar point of view maintained by some of the finest and most vital Christians in East Africa, namely the members of the Revival fellowship groups. Their attitude is derived from an honest acknowledgement of the hypocrisy and concealed wrong-doing which marked their own lives before their conversion, and which they know is common to all men apart from the newness of life which comes through salvation by Christ. Therefore, they argue, society will never be improved by social and political action, until the individual human lives which are the material of society have been purified from the sin which corrupts all systems and organizations. They believe that they are called, as Christians, not to repair or reconstruct the fabric of society but to live as a new community within society, calling men to join them in their experience of Christ, and demonstrating the quality of a supernatural fellowship in which there is neither Muganda nor Kikuyu, neither black nor white, neither civilized nor uneducated, neither male nor female. This, as we shall see in the next chapter, is a truly New Testament conception of the Church, but it is only part of the truth.

A Nigerian clergyman, reporting on his visit to Kenya in 1954, described his contacts with the Revival Christians who endured so magnificently the baffled fury of the Mau Mau till the whole world marvelled to see such faith:

We discovered among the 'brethren' of Kenya, under the Mau Mau tribulation, a sense of living only for the 'Other World'. One of them told me that he would think it useless to take part in the government of his country with a view to making it more righteous. To him government and the power it wields belong to this world, with which the 'sons of light' should have no parley. Perhaps the frustration caused by the social conditions of Kenya and the helpless condition in which people find themselves owing to the difficulties of the Emergency have influenced the speaker towards that position.[1]

But, though this is still the express belief of the Revival Movement, more and more men from those fellowship groups are in fact finding themselves led to positions of social and political responsibility, frequently because no one else is regarded as trustworthy where money or privilege is concerned. In 1954, for example, the Prime Ministers of two of the Kingdoms in Uganda were of the 'brethren'; and so are many of the best men in the public services to-day in East Africa. They do revolutionary things, such as reparation to Government or to mercantile houses or individuals for what was wrongfully taken in the past. Such behaviour challenges and changes societies.

The Methodist Church in the Gold Coast showed itself aware of this vital need, in calling all her members

to take the Christian witness of service into their daily life. In particular she calls those who have the requisite gifts to take upon themselves the responsibility of serving on Town Councils, Trade Unions, Education Committees, State Treasury Committees, Co-operative Societies, Political Organizations, Native Tribunals and Childrens' Courts, ever reminding them of their duty to bring to such tasks the mind of Christ.[2]

It would be a disaster for Africa at this time if those who are politically aware, and actively engaged in shaping their society, begin to drift away from the Church, in which so many of them have grown up, feeling that it is unsympathetic and condemnatory in its attitude towards their endeavours. There is in many countries a danger of this happening to an extent unparalleled even in Europe. But such a separation of religion and society would be clean contrary to all African tradition and feeling. Here, religion has always been thought of as permeating and supporting all the economic and social

1. Edmund Ilogu, *West Meets East* (Highway Press, 1955), pp. 20–1.
2. *The Church and the State* (Cape Coast, 1949).

activities of men, and especially as the source of the rulers' guidance and strength. In the early days of Christianity in many areas it was, for this reason, felt to be of tremendous importance that the new faith should be accepted by the King or the Chief. In the same way the colonial power was regarded as introducing a Christian government, so that British administration and Christian Mission were thought by the Africans to be intimately linked to a degree that would have surprised even the most devout of the old colonial administrators. Therefore, as an observer from the Central African Federation writes,

since it is assumed that the Church must have had some influence on the original Colonial policy for these parts, the African expects some guidance and help from the Church in a day when there seems to be some departure from the Colonial policy so long set forth and exemplified by phrases now set aside in favour of new ones. An attitude of silence from the Church leads to the conclusion by the African that the Church from overseas will always react in favour of its own nationals' aspirations, and consequently an urge is given to the separatist tendency in the African mind, and the desire grows to see the Church reflecting the aspirations of the indigenous inhabitants.

Out of this kind of disillusionment grow the separatist sects of Africa, some of which seek to combine a distorted Christianity with an aggressive and destructive nationalism.

A religion which is not related positively to the total developing life of the community will never do for Africa. But neither will a social gospel busily engaged in a programme of improvement which leaves the deep personal levels of human nature untransformed. The heart of the matter is the urgent need for a Church in Africa which is both supernatural and responsible, in the full meaning of both those words.

CHAPTER TWO

The Answer of the Bible

THE true God of the Bible is a God who is concerned with the events of history and active in them. 'I am the Lord thy God which brought thee out of the land of Egypt, out of the house of bondage. Thou shalt have none other gods before me' (Exodus 20. 2). What these opening words of the Ten Commandments really mean is: 'I am the God who has taken revolutionary action in history and brought into being a new nation; any other kind of God is a false one.'

The religion of the Bible is as much concerned with the things of this world as with the things of the world to come. It shows us quite clearly that *men*, and not only 'souls', are the object of God's love. God created man as a creature with soul and body mysteriously combined; Christ came to save the whole man, both soul and body; the Christian is called to offer both soul and body as his reasonable sacrifice, that both combined may be possessed by the Holy Spirit; and even in the world to come the body is not, according to Scripture, to be omitted from the final perfection in the glory of God. As Canon Fison has strikingly said: 'From the beginning of creation to the end of time the Christian faith is a materialistic faith.'[1]

God's call comes to men and women, not merely to souls. It is a call to respond and obey in the circumstances of this world. God calls men to be responsible for their community, to co-operate with Him in shaping the events of history, to strive to make the pattern of their society conform with the laws of His Kingdom. And this God who calls His people to obedient responsibility for this world, in spite of all setbacks, does not allow them to despair, but again and again promises that what He calls them to attempt He will enable them to achieve, if only they are faithful to their covenant with Him 'For this reason,' writes Professor Wright,

1. J. E. Fison, *The Christian Hope* (Longmans, 1954), p. 50.

complete pessimism regarding the world, which releases the called community from responsibility to withdrawal, is not possible. God has not withdrawn himself but is able and will do 'signs and wonders' for which we must diligently look and expectantly wait. Our responsibility is thus here in this life now, and there must be no evasion of it.[1]

It is of great significance that of all the regions of the world the place which God chose to be the scene of His dealing with a particular people – His laboratory, as it were, for demonstrating His nature and His way for all men – was Palestine. For that country has always been like a bridge with a great highway running across it. No place could have been more public. Whoever lived there could not possibly be cut off from the rest of the world; a policy of isolation was unthinkable. Although the Hebrews were called to be 'not of the world' spiritually, yet socially, economically, and politically they were bound to be completely 'in the world'. Israel could not be a self-sufficient nation, but was bound to depend on trade with her neighbours. She exchanged corn and oil for timber from Lebanon in order to build her cities. In her great days she bought horses from Asia Minor to sell them in Egypt, and her ships brought incense and gold from Southern Arabia for the trade with Assyria. So the Israelites were bound up with the culture of the surrounding nations. Their potters imitated the jars and bowls of Syria; their clothes were copied from the fashions of Mesopotamia; they were quick to introduce Greek lamps into their houses; even their temple was modelled on the architecture of Egypt. If God had wanted his Chosen People, and us who are their heirs in faith, to be disinterested and detached from the affairs of this world, He surely would have selected a more isolated retreat to be their earthly home.

The Laws of Moses, which were the basis of Hebrew religious life, show clearly that God's will for His people is not confined to their prayers and their personal holiness. The righteousness which God requires is a righteousness of the

1. G. Ernest Wright, *The Biblical Doctrine of Man in Society* (S.C.M., 1954), p. 137.

market place, of the law courts, of the palace, a righteousness affecting the policy of land tenure, the maintenance of public health, and the strategy of war. False measures and weights were strictly forbidden, and the prophets Amos and Micah both denounced the merchants of their day for dishonest trading (Leviticus 19. 35, 36; Amos 8. 5; Micah 6. 10, 11). Generous 'compassionate leave' was to be granted to soldiers (Deuteronomy 20. 5–9); and ruthless 'scorched-earth' tactics, such as Jehoshaphat employed against Moab (2 Kings 3. 19, 25), were contrary to the divine regulations (Deuteronomy 20. 19). Punishment for crime was to be just and severe, but never so severe as to cheapen human life (Deuteronomy 16. 18–20; 25. 2, 3); and the prophets constantly arraigned the judges and rulers for taking bribes and oppressing the poor (Amos 5. 12; Isaiah 10. 1, 2). The law made special humanitarian provision for the landless, and the prophets were stern in their denunciation of the growing class of landowners who accumulated huge estates by extortion or by mortgage from smallholders in financial difficulties (Isaiah 5. 8; Micah 2. 2; Nehemiah 5. 1–6).

Most striking is the prophets' sense of their responsibility with regard to the State, as represented by the King. Though, like other rulers of the ancient world, the King was to have almost unlimited power, yet in Israel the State could never be absolute, for the King, like any other man, was subject to the Law. That Law expressly forbade him to use his power for self-aggrandisement, for it was given him in order that he might champion the poor and be the supreme source of the well-being and peace of the common people (Deuteronomy 17. 14–20; Psalm 72). So high was the Hebrew ideal of kingship that out of their constant disappointment with human rulers grew their picture of the expected Messiah who at last would fulfil all their hopes of a perfect King.

The words of Samuel summarize the Old Testament conception of the duty of the 'Church' (or prophet) towards the 'State' (or King): 'God forbid that I should sin against the Lord in ceasing to pray for you: but I will instruct you in the good and right way' (1 Samuel 12. 23). That instruction was always available to those Kings who were humble enough to pay heed to it, and a long line of great prophets were unfailing in their responsibility to make known the will of God in the affairs of state. Samuel, Elisha, Isaiah, and Jeremiah, together with a goodly company of unnamed men of God, did not limit their advice to strictly 'religious' matters, but spoke the Word of the Lord also concerning political alliances and the strategy of war (2 Kings 6. 8–12; Isaiah 30. 1–5; Jeremiah 38. 14–28). The prophets' ministry to the State did not end with prayer and guidance. They were well aware of the innate tendency in all rulers to over-reach the bounds of authority and abuse power at the expense of liberty and individual right. This profound distrust of the State is expressed in Samuel's great speech when the people demanded a King (1 Samuel 8. 10–19); and the same insight led Ezekiel to omit the word 'King' from his utopian vision of the 'ideal society', and to use, instead, the word 'prince': i.e. viceroy, one subject to God as the ultimate Ruler (Ezekiel 46).

And so, in spite of the cowardly compromise of the State-supported domestic chaplains attached to the palace, there were never lacking men of courage who were prepared to resist the unlawful claims of the monarchy in the name of the God of righteousness. Nathan confronted David with his sin, not as an adulterer but as a tyrant who had abused his authority as King and commander-in-chief to rob the poor man of his 'one little ewe lamb' (2 Samuel 12. 1–15). In exactly the same way, Elijah denounced Ahab for assuming, as pagan Jezebel had done, that a King had a divine right to remove from his path anyone who dared to resist his absolute demands (1 Kings 21). Even in Israel there were those who protested that the spokesmen of religion had no right to interfere in politics (Amos 7. 12, 13); but these are the 'false prophets', and the Old Testament makes it abundantly clear that God's will includes a just order in the State and economic security for all subjects, and that those who know His will have a responsibility to proclaim it.

The knowledge of God's intention thus prevented the prophets from taking the simplest course open to them, namely, complete withdrawal from 'civilized' and increasingly complicated business life. Instead they pointed to the tension between people and God, called sin by its proper name, and rehearsed the fundamentals of the covenant faith. To live in the world meant a considerable risk: it involved the knowledge of God's judgment, of His 'Day', upon all the proud and haughty, and of the danger of losing all to find anything.[1]

When the dynasty of Omri, especially King Ahab and his Phoenician wife Jezebel, were trying to lead the Hebrew people away from the worship of the true God, the prophets, under the spiritual leadership of Elisha, actually plotted and carried out a revolution in which all the representatives of that dynasty in both Israel and Judah were killed (1 Kings 17 to 2 Kings 11). This was an extreme case, and the only time that such drastic measures were taken; seventy years later Hosea, the prophet of mercy, showed that he believed that this revolution had been wrong (Hosea 1. 4). None the less this incident illustrates how seriously the religious leaders of the Old Testament regarded their responsibility in the realm of social and political action.

If we had only the Old Testament we should be left in no doubt about the responsibility of the people of God to concern themselves with political and social, as well as religious and spiritual affairs. All through the history of the Church, and even in our own day, there have been some who have based their whole theory of social ethics on the Laws of Moses alone, and have hoped to persuade the State to enforce by a rule of law things that can only be the free resolve of faith. But we cannot do that now without distortion. The lessons we have already drawn from the Old Testament are still valid, as we shall see; but we shall not learn them aright unless we face honestly the problems raised by the Gospels. And when we turn to the New Testament we find certain very clear contrasts.

First, under the monarchy[2] the Hebrews were an independent nation, whereas the Jews after the Exile were a small

1. *Ibid.*, p. 146. 2. c. 1000 B.C.–586 B.C.

subject province in one or another of the great Empires. Perhaps this was one reason why, once the little Jewish national home had been restored, by the middle of the fifth century B.C., there were no more prophets. Similarly the Christians of New Testament times were a tiny minority in the Roman Empire, and had no voice in public affairs. The action of the prophets under the Kings of Israel may not be taken as a model for Christians in a subject state, either in the first or in the twentieth century.

Secondly, Israel was a theocracy; that is to say, the nation itself was ruled by God. One body of law governed both the religious community with its worship and the State with its institutions. The distinction between the Church and the nation had not been made in Israel before the time of Christ. Christians, on the other hand, have from the first had to face the problem of living in a secular State embracing different races and many creeds.

Thirdly, the law of righteousness of the Old Testament was superseded in the New not by another law but by a gospel. The disciples of Jesus ought to be distinguished from the Pharisees by a righteousness which exceeds all the demands which any law can make. In their relationships they are no longer to live on a basis of rights and dues, claims and duties, but on the basis of free grace and love. This way of life can, by its very nature, never be expressed in a code of laws or laid as a rule upon people outside the voluntary brotherhood of those who are committed to it. Christ's Kingdom is not of this world, and its law of love can never be made the law of the kingdoms of this world:

In this total setting aside of all that is and must be called justice in the things of this world the Gospel is revealed as the teaching which does not regulate earthly things but proclaims the Kingdom of God, and the justice which it proclaims is not the justice which is applicable to the circumstances of this world; it is the nature of the new aeon. This was stated by Jesus directly and explicitly. When a man came to Him asking Him to arbitrate in a dispute over his inheritance Jesus refused with the utmost sharpness, 'Man, who made me a judge or divider over you?' He does not say that there should be no judges and no just division of inheritances, but that it is not His business.[1]

But the New Testament does not suggest that the Christian Church is to remain outside and indifferent to the needs of society and the justice of this world. The heart of the life and teaching of Jesus was a voluntary acceptance of involvement with the life of this world, in order that by completely identifying himself with men in their society he might redeem both them and their society from sin. So He who was sinless underwent the baptism of repentance with other men. Unlike John the Baptist, who chose the way of separation from the world, Jesus came eating and drinking, and scandalized the religious leaders by being so normal. He stated most clearly this principle of voluntary involvement, when He paid the statutory tax for the upkeep of the Temple (Matthew 17. 24–27). Those who by faith in Him had become sons of God and heirs of God's Kingdom were in the truest sense independent of the institutions and organizations of this world; but, 'lest we cause them to stumble', they were to submit to those claims in common with all other men as fellow members of the one society. Though He came to call men into a Kingdom that could only be entered by the new birth, a Kingdom whose politics, like its peace, were not of this world, yet that Kingdom was meant to be as leaven in the midst of human society, and its subjects, though citizens of heaven, were called not to withdrawal but to responsibility as citizens of the world.

So, although Jesus had come to inaugurate a new humanity with a new kind of relationship, He was not indifferent to the world of men as he found it.

This responsibility of Christ, and His followers, towards the world of men as they found it, was a two-fold responsibility of judgement and creative participation: *creative participation*, because God had chosen the way of Incarnation and intended to save the world by being involved in it;

1. Emil Brunner, *Justice and the Social Order* (Lutterworth Press, 1945), p. 103. It is from the 14th chapter of his book that most of the foregoing argument is derived.

judgement, because there had come into the world a new humanity with a new relationship, in the light of which old things were seen to be passing away and all their values to be only relative (John 12. 31).

The judgement of Christ upon the institutions of His day embraced a great many different groups and was always somewhat unexpected. Amid the fierce nationalism of His time, He did not throw in his lot with the 'men of violence' who were attempting to 'take the Kingdom of Heaven by storm'. Yet neither did He denounce them; He warned that 'they who take the sword shall perish by the sword'; but at least one former revolutionary, Simon the Zealot, was numbered among his disciples. Neither did He attack, as might have been expected, the Herodian party who favoured collaboration with the Imperial power, though He clearly despised their hypocrisy and the treachery of 'that fox', Herod (Mark 12. 15; Luke 13. 32).

He judged the overbearing power of the Roman rulers (Mark 10. 42), who represented themselves as the 'bene-factors' of the subject races (Luke 22. 25); and, holding in His hand the coin which bore the Emperor's image and the inscription 'Tiberius Caesar son of Augustus the god', He made that superb distinction between the rights of God and the relative rights of the State: 'Render unto Caesar the things that are Caesar's and unto God the things that are God's' (Mark 12. 15–17). On the other hand, He rejected the ideas of race which went with his people's nationalism, and incurred their bitterest resentment on account of His attitude to foreigners (Luke 4. 25–30, 10. 33; John 4. 9). But His most powerful denunciation was reserved for the social and religious leaders of His own people. No Old Testament prophet spoke with more direct vehemence than Jesus in His tremendous accusation of the scribes and Pharisees (Matthew 23; Luke 20. 45–47). And it was against the corrupt family of the High Priests that He directed his only act of public interference with an existing institution, when He broke up the market which was organized in the Temple under the licence of Annas himself (Mark 11. 15–18).

This ministry of judgement of the existing order was exercised also by the first Christians, who therefore were instructed not to submit their own disputes to the judgement of pagan lawcourts (1 Corinthians 6. 1–4). In the light of this critical insight they saw the power of Rome, at the end of the century, for what it was, a Satanic beast and the enemy of Christ (Revelation 13). Paul was exercising such Christian judgement when he exposed the injustice of the magistrates at Philippi (Acts 16. 35–39); and Peter and John showed the authorities in Jerusalem the true grounds for their disobedience, in the words, 'We must obey God rather than men' (Acts 4. 19, 5. 29). In later centuries thousands of Christians gave their lives in this selfsame resistance to the State, when they judged that it was usurping the authority of God and claiming an absolute and total right over the lives and destinies of men. And in our own day the roll of such martyrs is being steadily increased.

But, as Professor Wright explains, 'the Christian responsibility of judgement ... involves an active, positive, and responsible role in the world's life'.[1] The divinely ordained place of government in this world is recognized by Paul in the well-known passage in Romans 13. 1–7, where he teaches that the responsible role of the Christian in relation to the government is dutiful and obedient citizenship, not only through fear of punishment, 'but also for conscience sake'. Civil government in Paul's view is part of the natural order of a moral universe. Just as nature will usually reward the skilful, hard-working farmer and starve the slacker and the fool; just as laxity and corruption in a people must bring forth social degradation and collapse; so civil government, as part of the same natural moral order, exists to reward honesty and punish wrongdoing. The State belongs to the realm of nature, not to the realm of grace; but God is the God of nature as well as of grace. Even when the Roman State had outlawed the Christian Church and persecution was beginning, the duty of loyalty to the Empire was still being insisted upon (1 Peter 2. 13–17); and Paul from his

1. Wright, *op. cit.*, p. 150.

Roman prison commanded Timothy to maintain in the Church regular prayer for those in authority (1 Timothy 2. 1, 2).

We may sum up this aspect of the teaching of the Bible by remembering that it is the nature of the Church in society both to be different and to be involved. This was beautifully expressed in a letter written in the second century A.D. by an unknown Christian to an enquirer called Diognetus:

What the soul is in the body, thus Christians are in the world. The soul is spread through all parts of the body; so are Christians through all the cities of the world. The soul lives in the body but is not of the body; so Christians live in the world but are not of the world . . . The soul is shut up in the body but itself holds the body together; so too Christians are held down in the world yet it is they who hold the world together.

First, then, the Church must be different and detached. Unless the Christian community is in fact living on a different level, according to different standards, from the rest of society: unless it enjoys a peculiar and more honest fellowship in its relationships, and has an extraordinary unselfishness and a supernatural love in its activities: then it is not being the true Church and has nothing specifically Christian to contribute to the State. 'If the salt hath lost its savour, wherewith shall it be salted?' (Matthew 5. 13).

Secondly, in its involvement, the Church has to bring both judgement and creative participation to the society in which it lives. In the light both of the New Testament and of the witness of the prophets in the Old, we can set out as follows the duties of the Church and its members towards the State.

JUDGEMENT

1. To hold before men in their legislative, administrative, and juridical tasks the standards of righteousness and justice which alone exalt a nation.
2. To lend moral support to the State when it upholds those standards, and to criticize it fearlessly when it departs from them.

3. To be an ever-present reminder to the State that it exists only as the servant of God and of man, and that its authority is only relative.

PARTICIPATION

1. To pray for the State, its people and its government.
2. Loyally to obey the State and to pay whatever is due in taxes and service; to disobey only if obedience would be clearly contrary to God's will.
3. To co-operate wholeheartedly with the State in promoting the welfare of its citizens and in removing social, economic, and civic wrongs.
4. To permeate the public mind with the spirit of righteousness and brotherhood, and to train up Christian men and women who can bring whole and stable personalities to the service of the community.

It is true, of course, that the Bible does make mention of a few sects of people who felt called to separate themselves completely from the ordinary life of the world, usually in some sort of religious community or brotherhood. Such were the Nazarites (Numbers 6. 1–8), the Rechabites (Jeremiah 35), and the Jewish Covenanters, whose old scrolls have recently been found hidden in a cave by the Dead Sea. So also through all the history of the Church there have been communities who have been called to a life of complete withdrawal from the economic structure and the general culture of the society around them, as a witness to the true values and the eternal riches which are spiritual. But they have always been a minority; and the Church as a whole has never believed that it should withdraw in that way, but rather that it was called to obey and serve God in the context of all the daily demands and responsibilities of family, neighbourhood, and nation. The long roll of the great Christian statesmen and reformers, without whose sacrificial witness all the best elements in our civilization would be lacking, is evidence that the Church in past centuries was wide awake to its responsibilities in the world.

It is remarkable also that genuine revival in the Church

has always led to a renewed sense of its 'worldly' responsibilities. This was wonderfully demonstrated in the great movement inspired by John Wesley in the eighteenth century. The men who were converted in the course of that movement of the Spirit were the very men who set on foot the most concentrated and far-reaching series of social and political reforms that the world has ever seen in so short a space of time. It has been well said that

within a lifetime, like a group of mountain springs, there appeared in England a series of religious and humanitarian movements which altered the whole course of English history, influenced most of Europe and affected the life of three other continents.[1]

This principle of responsibility has in fact inspired a very great deal of the activity of the Church in Africa up to the present time. Alfred Tucker, the great Bishop of Uganda, is an outstanding, but by no means isolated example of missionary concern for every new economic and sociological development which would alter the pattern of the lives of the people whom God had committed to his charge. He battled indomitably for what he believed was politically right, and had a considerable share in bringing about the establishment of the British Protectorate in Uganda. He showed a most responsible awareness of what was going to be the effect upon his people of the building of the railway from Mombasa to Lake Victoria and the imposition of the universal hut tax. He and his fellow missionaries launched a staggering programme of educational development; they introduced hospital and maternity services into the country; they provided widespread facilities for training in craft and industrial work; they attempted to establish a trading company inspired by Christian ideals, and one of them was responsible for the introduction of cotton as a smallholders' cash crop, which was more than anything else going to improve the whole standard of life of the people.

This is a familiar story, and it can be paralleled elsewhere in Africa; but the deep sense of responsibility for the whole

1. E. M. Howse, *Saints in Politics* (Allen and Unwin, 1952), p. 7.

of life which was the motive of all this concern has not always been clearly recognized by later generations of Christians in Africa. Bishop Tucker summed up the true objective of his manifold activities as 'the equipment of the whole man for the battle of life', and, in particular, 'the great work of fitting the Baganda for the demands which would be made upon them as they came in contact with the outside world'.[1]

A considerable part of this 'equipment of the whole man for the battle of life' has been provided in the opportunities offered by the Church for first-hand experience of responsible self-government. Not all Missions were equally eager to put the reins of Church government into African hands, but sooner or later almost all have come to accept the wisdom of those bolder pioneers who had the vision and the faith to trust the truly indigenous Church. Again Bishop Tucker's words are worth quoting:

It should ever be the object of those whose God-given task it is to assist in the building up of a native Church, to develop in the Councils of that Church independence and initiative. This, I believe, will best be done by throwing the fullest possible responsibility upon the native organization. A realized sense of responsibility will quicken into life powers and qualities which, duly exercised, will in course of time bear whatever burden may be put upon them in the way of administration and government.[2]

There is no doubt at all that again and again the organs of Church government have been the training grounds of African leadership, which has extended into all kinds of responsibility in spheres beyond the Church's institutions. From the earliest days Christians have played a leading part in local government and in the civil service.

But these principles, accepted so often by the pioneers, need to be remembered in our own day and carried much further. The Church, which has already acted responsibly in the fields of education, medicine and, to a lesser extent, those of agriculture and social welfare, should now be encouraging

1. Alfred Tucker, *Eighteen Years in Uganda* (Arnold, 1908), Vol. ii, pp. 263–4.
2. *Ibid.*, Vol. ii, p. 148.

its members to enter with the same high calling into the fields of co-operative organization, trade unionism, and political journalism. The Church, which has in the past encouraged its adherents to take on chieftainships and play their part in local government, should to-day give the same encouragement to its members to participate responsibly on central legislative bodies and in the emergent political parties.

Is it true that the African Church has less courage to-day in this respect than it had half a century ago? It has been said of some of the teachers in the Church's secondary schools in Kenya:

They were sometimes impatient about the rate of progress tolerated by the leaders of State, Church, and nation. In one place there was an indication that these young men were not being fully used in the running of the school. They do lack experience which comes only from many years of teaching and management. But they possess vision without which the nation will perish. It would be a tragedy if their zeal and vision were submerged under tardy traditions and conservatism.[1]

Of course, there are risks involved in responsibility; and in the arena of national politics there are dangers of a most subtle kind, and a terrifying battery of temptations. But the Church must never avoid temptation merely by shifting the responsibility on to others. Some one must stand in the place of spiritual danger; then who better than the Christian? And if the Church is to be true to the whole teaching of the Bible, and to the long tradition of its past centuries, then it must be sending forth its sons and daughters into all the places of deepest responsibility in the nation's life; and those whom it sends forth it must support with the strong arm of fellowship and prayer. When that happens the Church will again be able to praise her Lord, who having called us to His service, even on the most hazardous frontiers, can make us worthy of our calling: 'For that the leaders took the lead in Israel, for that the people offered themselves willingly, bless ye the Lord' (Judges 5. 2).

1. Ilogu, *op. cit.*, p. 8.

CHAPTER THREE

Church and State

EVERY man is born into a community. He is a member of a family and he grows up inheriting certain family characteristics, certain property, certain obligations; he learns certain family traditions, certain patterns of behaviour, certain points of pride. In the same way, also, he is a member of a particular clan, tribe, and nation, and these will give him a particular culture and history, a particular way of looking at things, probably a particular religion. It is in such ways that every human being belongs to his own environment. He has his roots in a particular soil; he cannot be transplanted to a different soil without feeling the change very deeply; and if he is left with his roots in no soil his personality will become weak and unhappy and sick. Men and women who do not live in a community and feel that they really belong to it are not completely human. Something essential is missing, something which God has ordained for them as necessary for their true life. 'It is not good that the man should be alone' (Genesis 2. 18).

From this two other truths follow, which we must also believe to be the law of God for man's life in this world. First, every man must learn to live happily together with his neighbour. Secondly, a man cannot pick and choose who his neighbours will be. His community – whether it is family, or village or nation – consists of *the people who are there*, not merely the people whom he would choose as his companions. He therefore has to find a way of living together with all sorts of people, including those whom he does not like, those with whom he disagrees, those whose interests are different from, or opposed to his own.

When two brothers quarrel it is not often possible for one of them to leave home and live somewhere else. They have to find some way of settling their quarrel in order to go on living in one family. So also in a village the man with a large herd of cattle may find that his interests clash with the man who is trying to grow a large field of cotton, and they will have to find some way of settling their dispute, so that the cows can go to their grazing without trampling on the cotton. We read in the Bible that the herdsmen of Abraham quarrelled with the herdsmen of his nephew Lot, and they settled the dispute very simply by going to different areas of Palestine. They were fortunate to live in a primitive society when the population was very small and most people were nomads. But at a later period when the children of Israel were occupying Palestine we find that disputes over land could not be settled so easily; quarrels had to be dealt with by judges, and a complicated system of laws had to be drawn up concerning property. In an organized community there are bound to be differences of interest between individuals, or between clans, or between groups engaged in different trades. Then there will be the need for some way of dealing with the conflict and maintaining good order and a united community. So arises the need for the State.

The members of a community do not live as separate individuals, but are constantly forming themselves into a great variety of different groups to satisfy different needs. The inhabitants of two villages on opposite sides of a river may combine together to build a bridge. The cocoa or coffee growers of a certain district may form a co-operative to market their crops and bargain for the best prices. Such organized groups do not simply happen; some members have to be chosen and recognized as leaders, and their authority is obeyed by common consent. At certain times this kind of organization for mutual benefit has to be carried out on a much wider scale, especially in times of emergency. If the emergency is a national one, such as famine or invasion, then there must be a nation-wide organization, with authority given to someone by common consent. The Bible tells us, again, how when the whole nation of Egypt was threatened with famine, authority was given to Joseph to commandeer the entire corn crop for seven years in order to store it so that rations could be distributed during the famine. That sort of nation-wide organization for common welfare can never be achieved except by some recognized ruler or rulers who have authority to give orders and to punish those who refuse to obey.

In a highly developed society this organization for welfare is not limited to emergency regulations, such as famine relief or defence. Or rather, it might be said that in a complex and highly populated society the necessity for detailed planning and control presents a permanent state of emergency, so that many kinds of amenity – roads, schools, medical services, welfare facilities, agricultural and trade organizations, which could once be entrusted to voluntary, local associations – may now become the responsibility of a central or regional authority, knowing all the needs and integrating all these activities into a single plan. The State therefore has a twofold task: it has to maintain order and it has to promote welfare. Both these responsibilities have always been recognized by every State; but the special conditions of our highly complex and overcrowded modern communities have produced the need for what we call the Welfare State.

So that the two needs for order and welfare can be met, the State has to make rules for the whole of the community and it has to enforce them effectively by some system whereby the law-breaker is punished. The community recognizes a small group, or a single individual, within its midst as the central authority to whom is given this special task of making and enforcing the laws. This central authority we call 'the government'.

The government, whether it is a King or Chief ruling with absolute authority as sole law-maker and judge, or a group of aristocratic elders inheriting by birth the privilege of rule, or a complicated legislative assembly of representatives elected by the people, can only effectively carry out its real task when the people of the whole community consent to its rule. All good government is government by consent. This is not to say that all good government is necessarily democratic. That is a different question altogether, which we shall face in a later chapter. An absolute monarch may rule with the enthusiastic consent of the people and has often done so in many different lands. Even acquiescence is a form of consent. In every country there are large numbers of people who care nothing for politics; they will obey the laws, if they know them, without much grumbling, and though they are not actively enthusiastic, neither are they inwardly opposed. The majority of people in Africa have given that sort of consent to the colonial government in their territory until fairly recently.

But any government unsupported by consent is a form of tyranny. This is obviously true in any of the totalitarian States, in which the majority of the people would change their government if they could, and obey only because they are afraid. In a much less obvious way it is true even in some of the democracies of Western Europe, in which every year more and more regulations are made by civil servants in government departments, to whose powers the people have never consented because they have never heard of them. In such societies a citizen is liable to discover at any moment that he is a lawbreaker, or that his liberties have been curtailed; when he does discover it, he is surprised and protests violently, but it is then too late. The power has been quietly wielded without the public's knowledge. That kind of tyranny may develop out of bureaucracy – the rule of civil servants.

Whether it is of the obvious totalitarian pattern, or the more respectable, insidious type of rule by officialdom, government without the consent of the governed is always bad government, because it means that the State and the community are set in opposition to each other. The power of the government then rests upon force alone; and the obedience of the people is based on fear of the penalties rather than respect for the community. The State is thought of as the oppressive 'they', and lawbreaking is no longer regarded as wrong but only as risky. Those who are clever enough will break the law, and public morality will not blame them. So the community grows more truculent and subversive, and the State reacts by becoming more repressive. A government which tends to produce such a relationship of hostility with the community is failing to fulfil the two functions of the State, namely, to maintain order and to promote welfare.

The Christian view of the State, as we have already seen, accepts all this, regarding civil government as part of the will of God for mankind as expressed in the natural order of a moral universe. The State exists for the common good of the people, although its authority is not derived merely from the people's will but from the will of God. It holds its power as delegated by God. If therefore it is to carry out its divinely ordained task aright, the supreme thing in all its legislation and administration is that it should be guided not by popular approval but by justice. A government in which the rulers are all the time, as it were, looking over their shoulders to see whether the people are pleased with them is likely to fall short of true justice almost as much as a government in which the rulers are abusing their power to forward their own private interests. In any good government the rulers should be in power by the people's consent, but that power is to be used to legislate for righteousness, not for popularity.

Whether they know it or not, rulers are responsible primarily to God to do *His* will in promoting the welfare of His children. This is true not only of a so-called 'Christian State'. Any State, whatever the beliefs of its members, is subservient to a power higher than itself. The State is never an end in itself, but a means to an end; it exists for the sake of the community, not for its own sake; we must not forget that its highest officials are often called 'ministers', which means servants. If this is the true nature of the task of government, then it is clear that it can only be carried out by men who have learnt to put the needs of the community before their own interests, who have a strong sense of right and wrong, and who feel that they themselves, even more than those they govern, are subject to the demands of the laws of God.

We can now see the many differences between the nature and functions of the State and the Church. It is, however, so

39

important to grasp these clearly that it is worth setting them out in a series of contrasts.

1. The State must include in its responsibility every member of the community within its own boundaries; and every member of the community, without exception, is subject to the State. The Church, on the other hand, is a voluntary association or a number of associations, embracing only a particular group within the community.

2. The individual State is confined to its own national boundaries, and is concerned with the government of those within its frontiers, and with its relations with other sovereign states beyond them. The Church on the other hand is a universal fellowship which transcends the limits of particular States, and is concerned with God's will for the whole world.

3. The State is ordained to maintain justice, security, and relative well-being among sinful men and women in an evil world. The Church is ordained to preach a Gospel of salvation from sin and evil, and to demonstrate a fellowship in which they are being overcome.

4. The State must deal with the immediate factors in a changing scene; its political decisions therefore must be accommodated to a particular concrete situation. The Church, however, is called to witness to eternal realities. Its standard, being set by God Himself, cannot be altered to fit in with changing circumstances.

5. The State is primarily concerned with providing the external framework for the good life; and therefore it must deal with man's visible actions, and can use law and, if need be, force, to coerce men. The Church is primarily concerned with the inward springs and motives of the good life, and therefore its distinctive method is patient persuasion and, if need be, suffering.

Yet when we have clearly understood the different callings of State and Church we must not fail to recognize that both are ordained by God. Both are dealing with a world in which men through selfishness and sin are liable to spoil one another's lives; the State exists by the will of God as part of

His way of dealing with this situation; the Church also exists by the will of God as a different part of His way of dealing with it. The State is not an end in itself, but neither is the Church. On different levels both are to be seen as means to an end and both are responsible to God as His servants, called into being for the sake of His children. The leaders of both are always to think of themselves, therefore, as 'ministers' and 'stewards'. The individual Christian is a member both of the State and the Church, each of which is an organized community inviting the co-operation of its members in the furtherance of its tasks. He has his duty, therefore, to be both a good citizen and a good Christian, believing that in both capacities he is obeying the call of God.

Of course, the relationship between Church and State will differ considerably in different countries according to the attitude of the State towards all voluntary associations, and to the Christian Church in particular. Moreover, such variations will be reflected in the reaction of the Church, which, in different historical situations, may be called to criticize or even to oppose those in authority. The State may be openly anti-religious, or specifically anti-Christian, or it may be neutralist and secular; it may be keenly Islamic or Hindu or Buddhist; it may be professedly pro-Christian, or it may support one branch of the Christian Church to the exclusion of others. Again, where there is an established relationship between a particular State and a particular Church it may take a variety of forms according to the past history of the country concerned. So, for example, the Church-State relationship is very different in England, Scotland, and Portugal. There are some sharp contrasts of policy even in British colonies. In Uganda the Government has constitutionally established the position of the Anglican, the Roman Catholic, and the Moslem communities in their relationship with the State; in the north of Nigeria and of the Gold Coast, the Government has tended to discourage the spread of the Christian Church; while in British Somaliland Christian Missions are entirely forbidden.

The Church must recognize that while usually the attitude

of the State is beyond its control, in some cases the reaction of the government has been determined by the irresponsible behaviour of Christians. For example, the poor regard of the government of Israel for Christian Missions to-day largely results from the activities of the innumerable small sects which have appeared since the war in and around Jerusalem. And quite often governments grow impatient with the complications of dealing with a Church which is not one but many Churches. The true and best relationship between Church and State can never be realized until there is One Church.

Nevertheless, in spite of these varieties of degree in the relationship between them, it is still possible to recognize that both Church and State are the servants of God and responsible to Him. Neither is responsible to the other. The Church is not to be regarded as a department of the State, and the State should never be dominated by the Church. But both can, if they will, support one another in their complementary tasks and each can keep the other from going wrong.

For example, the State, because it must hold the supreme power in the community, is always tempted to exalt itself into an absolute and to claim to have the final word in ordering the destinies of its citizens. In the name of efficiency and order it can seek to turn individuals into the tools of the State instead of regarding the State as the servant of society. The Church can serve the State by checking this inevitable tendency before it goes too far. The Church has a plain duty to seek whether by any way it can bring to the notice of the State this divine insight, which is the Word of God to men. The truth which it is bound to proclaim was well summarized by the Oxford Conference on Church, Community, and State in 1937, which drew together a large number of Christian leaders from many walks of life and from all over the world:

We recognize the State as being in its own sphere the highest authority. It has the God-given aim in that sphere to uphold law and order and to minister to the life of its people. But as all authority

42

is from God, the State stands under His judgement. God is Himself the source of justice of which the State is not lord but servant. The Christian can acknowledge no ultimate authority but God: his loyalty to the State is part of his loyalty to God and must never usurp the place of that primary and only absolute loyalty.[1]

One aspect of the self-idolatry of the State which the Church must particularly guard against is the presumption of supposing that, as arbiter of the whole of life for its citizens, the State is responsible for their spiritual welfare also. Many countries of the 'West' as well as some in the East have a Minister or Government department responsible for religious affairs; and while it is justifiable for the State to keep in touch with the activities of religious bodies as much as with those of other voluntary agencies, yet in any such official appointment there is an inherent danger of progressive interference with the spiritual liberty of its citizens. The Christian Conference of Eastern Asia, which was convened at Bangkok in December 1949, referred specifically to this danger, saying:

We also are concerned about the trend in certain nations for the State to assume responsibility for the organization of the religious life, which is the province of religious communities and not of the State.[2]

On the other hand the State may be threatened not by pride, but by cynicism and despair. It not infrequently happens that statesmen who initiated a programme of social reform with high hopes and ideals have become so baffled by the complexities of the problems, so frustrated by the weaknesses and evil intentions of men, that a hopeless paralysis is induced. Such men may become exceedingly bitter, and from extreme idealism may swing violently into the basest materialism and self-interest. This reaction may be met in some African political leaders, whose bitter and negative policies result not from the rebuffs of racialism, bad as those may have been, but from the sheer disappointment and

1. *The Churches Survey Their Task* (Allen & Unwin, 1937), p. 60.
2. *The Christian Prospect in Eastern Asia* (Friendship Press, New York, 1950), p. 117.

frustration of years of fruitless effort to realize the worthy ideals with which they started. The same is true also of a number of white politicians in South Africa, where they say that the African's bitterest opponent is the liberal who has been let down. It is precisely at such points that the Church can best serve the State, with its proclamation that God is sovereign over the whole world.

A Kikuyu student at the University College of East Africa remarked to a European friend: 'I suppose it is the right of every young man to believe in the future of his country, but I can see no future any way for mine.' In contrast to that, a few months later another young Kikuyu leader, addressing a gathering of fellow Christians in the 'Torchbearer' movement said: 'The great thing about us is that we can look forward.' The busy politician may be tempted to disregard such a claim as the irresponsible idealism of men who know nothing of practical affairs. But in fact the claim is made the more confidently by those Christians who have themselves wrestled with the hard facts of the modern world. The 1937 Oxford Conference reported boldly that:

Christianity sincerely professed brings to those who are striving for a better order of society the serene confidence that to them that love God all things work together for good. This world is God's world. His Spirit is alive to-day as yesterday. . . . If men will put themselves unreservedly and humbly at the service of God He is able to overrule their stupidity and sin and to use them to set forward His purpose for mankind, which is a society better than their deserving as it is beyond their desires.[1]

Christian hope however marches in step with Christian realism; and here again the Church may serve the State by witnessing to the fact of man's natural sinfulness and so putting a curb on the ambitious and exaggerated promises made by political parties or by leaders hungry for popular support. The Christian leaders of East Asia, speaking of new political structures in the countries which had achieved, or were moving towards, their independence, said that political movements would have to be 'redeemed both of their

1. *The Churches Survey Their Task*, p. 129.

44

idolatrous and of their utopian pretensions in order to be of true service to man in the social and political order'.[1]

A fourth sphere in which the Church's witness to the State may help to guide it aright is that of inter-racial and inter-territorial relationships. The Church is a community which embraces all races and transcends all frontiers. In a given situation it may wholeheartedly support the national aspirations of a people, and approve of slogans which insist on African rights. But the Church must always be tempering these enthusiasms with its reminder of the rights of other nations and other races. It must ever oppose the dictum, 'My country right or wrong', and must bring home to the State as far as it is able that 'patriotism is not enough', but that the individual State, not being itself the ultimate political unit, is a member of a `family of nations, with international relationships, duties and rights which it is the responsibility of all good citizens to respect.

But this 'ministry of correction' between Church and State does not only work one way. There have been many times in history when the Church, invested with power, has been corrupted by it; and in these days no less than in the past, when the Church occupies an important place in any community, it may be tempted to exercise more control over social life than God intends. In such circumstances the State, under the providence of God, can perform the useful office of checking ecclesiastical pretensions and excesses, and if the Church is abusing its freedom or its privileges the State may rightly curtail them. When the Anglican and Roman Catholic factions were fighting each other for the control of Buganda in the 1890s, the State, as represented by Capt. Lugard, was clearly the agent of God in bringing to an end their disgraceful hostilities. And in the early days of the Christian Mission in Nyasaland the British government clearly did right to interfere with the autocratic power of a few eccentric missionaries who in the name of the Church were flagrantly abusing their authority over individual Africans in their charge.

1. *Christ – the Hope of Asia* (Madras, 1953), p. 32.

45

The fruitful interaction of Church and State is most evident when both cooperate in a particular task. There are many remarkable examples of this partnership in Africa, notably in the field of education and some of the other social services. In these joint activities Church and State can serve one another by keeping each other up to the mark. The State, for example, must insist that in its schools the Church does not fall below standard, while the Church must for ever be on guard against materialism or the worship of numbers in the educational policies of the State.

But if this mutual ministry of correction is to continue, two things are especially required: leadership and independence. If Church and State are to feel a continual tension, and yet accept it with an understanding of its value and with respect for one another, then each will need to have strong, clear-headed, and responsible leadership. Christians should aim at providing leaders in both, who will be able to work together fruitfully, both because they acknowledge a common Lord and also because they recognize the different function and calling of Church and State as servants of God. Moreover, in order to fulfil their calling, the essential difference and tension between Church and State must never be diminished or weakened by compromise. The State has most truly been called 'Caesar the beloved enemy', and if ever the element of opposition between the demands of Church and State should disappear it would be a serious disaster for both.

There is, therefore, always a grave danger when the Church becomes financially dependent on the State. While we recognize the benefits that have resulted from the partnership of Church and State in the field of education, for example, we must faithfully ensure that government grants are never allowed to buy the acquiescence of the Church in policies of which it cannot approve. No Church should ever accept financial grants which it is not prepared to relinquish immediately if ever the conditions attached to them make it impossible to exercise its positive, constructive, and critical function towards the State. The terrible dilemma which faces the Church in South Africa, in respect of its schools, should convince us that this is no simple problem with an obvious solution. For the Church does not, any more than the State, apply its principles in a vacuum, but always in the complexities of a concrete situation; and splendid moral gestures, like the closing of Church schools, can only be made at the expense of a vast number of dependent people. All the Church's covenants with Caesar must be conditional, and the Church has no right so to build its life on the basis of government aid that it is not ready at any moment to dispense with it. Such a relationship with the State can only be maintained by a Church which is at any moment prepared for sacrifice. The Church can only dare to face Caesar if it has already faced the Cross.

This 'facing of the Cross' must be shared by the ordinary Church members. There is a great need for all Christ's common people to be more clearly instructed in the real nature of the Kingdom of God and of the Welfare State, for in Africa there is much confusion between the two, and consequently much disillusionment. A Church which has really understood its terms of reference, which has counted the cost and grasped the truth that here it has no abiding city, may be a small Church, but one which is set free from anxiety and compromise, to be indeed the Body of Christ in the world.

The problem confronts the Church in its most acute form in those countries where its very existence appears to depend on keeping silence when its Lord is calling it to speak. This may be the case in some Islamic States, and also, to some extent, for the Protestant Churches in Madagascar and the Portuguese African territories. There indeed the Church is under the Cross. But the unequivocal call of Christ is clear. It might be summed up in the words of the Central Committee of the World Council of Churches in 1949:

We warn the Churches in all lands against the danger of being exploited for worldly ends. In the countries where the State is antagonistic to the Christian religion, or indeed wherever full religious freedom is denied, we ask all Christians to remember that the liberty which they receive from their Lord cannot be taken away by the violence or threat of any worldly power, or destroyed by suffering. Therefore we urge the Churches to bear clear corporate witness to the truth in Christ, and their ministers to continue to preach the whole Gospel.[1]

One point needs to be stressed, which will set all the foregoing argument in its true perspective. It is necessary to remember that in most territories of British Africa there are, in one sense or another, *two* governments. Already, under the principle of Indirect Rule, there is the native administration with its own local responsibilities, and there is the central colonial government; but more important still is the dualism between the present 'trustee State' and the 'successor State' of the future, whether the latter is to be African, or multiracial. The principles of the Church's relationship to the State, as outlined in this chapter, must be equally true and binding whatever the constitution of the State may be. At the present time, in many territories, the desire for self-government is such a burning issue that it is only too easy to concentrate on the Church's relationship to the colonial government, and to forget that there are equal problems in the Church's relationships to the emergent autonomous State of the future, even in its present condition of growth and struggle.

Both African and non-African Christians need to examine themselves honestly to find out whether they are willing for their Church to be just as critical of, and just as cooperative with, the government of their country, whether it be the colonial government of to-day or the independent government, of whatever sort, to which they are looking forward. The true Church belongs neither to the present nor to the future, but to Christ. It must judge every situation and make its decisions according to the standard of the Word of God and the mind of Christ, and not from any sense of expediency in the present, nor from a fear of prejudicing its future reputation when the 'successor' government takes over. Some Christians, for example, both African and non-

1. *Minutes and Reports* of the Second Meeting of the Central Committee of the World Council of Churches, 1949.

African, may be too reluctant for the Church ever to voice its criticism of colonial administration for fear of being considered subversive and disloyal; while in the same territory other Christians may be equally unwilling for the Church to approve the existing administration or to criticize the government's opponents, lest its actions be thought to involve it in 'imperialism'. Only a Church whose absolute loyalty to Christ has set it free from the consideration of men's good or bad opinion is truly able to serve the State by bringing to bear upon its problems the wisdom which is from above. For the beginning of that wisdom is the fear of the Lord which casts out all other fears.

CHAPTER FOUR

Political Action by the Church

'WHY doesn't the Church do something about it?' This is a question that is frequently asked by the critics of Christianity, more especially by those who have a particular axe to grind and are disappointed that the officials of the Church do not more enthusiastically assist them in that process. On the other hand there is always a minority who complain bitterly that the Church is 'interfering' in matters that are not its concern.

Both kinds of critic are, of course, making the very common mistake of limiting 'the Church' to its official leaders and organs only. We need constantly to remind ourselves that the work and witness of the Christian Church include the daily living and humble example of every Christian man, woman, and child, throughout the world. So also in the social and political field the Church's contribution is being made by a countless number of Christian people who are journalists, social workers, civil servants, local administrators, or members of legislative councils and assemblies; it is made by Christians who speak at meetings, who organize local branches of societies for social improvement, who write letters to the press; it is made by every Christian who casts his vote. In view of this it is clearly absurd to say that the Church either does not, or ought not to, play any part in politics.

And yet, while this book is mainly concerned with what individual lay Christians should be doing outside the precincts of the organized Churches considered as institutions, there is a limited sense in which the Church in its corporate life and through its official organs has a witness to bear and a work to do for the State and for national well being. It is this limited responsibility of the Church as a corporate association which we shall consider in this chapter, taking five main aspects in turn.

(1) First, the Church has the task of prayer. This is both individual and corporate. Every Christian as an individual should include in his private prayers regular intercession for his society and nation, especially remembering those in positions of responsibility in government, in industry, in education, and so on. If as an individual he feels strongly that a particular line of policy should be followed, or a much needed reform made law, it is perfectly natural and right that he should pray that the thing he believes to be right shall be brought to pass. As in all his prayer, however, he must recognize that his own judgement is fallible; and his desire must be submitted to the overruling petition that God's will be done. Providing that this condition is observed, there is nothing objectionable or ludicrous in the fact that sincere Christians may in their hopes and in their private devotions be opposing their prayers, as it were, one against another, for all their human aspirations are purified and reconciled in the will of Him unto whom all desires are known.

The public prayers of the Church, as the outward and visible body of believers, must be representative of the deep convictions of all the members of that Body. They cannot lightly be committed to the support of this or that side in any disagreement, and any attempt to exploit the prayers of Christians as a political weapon must be firmly resisted by all leaders in the Church. An example of this occurred in the Gold Coast in 1949, when the Churches refused to commemorate by national prayer the death of a demonstrator killed by police a year earlier, for that would have enabled some people to make political capital out of a religious occasion. More recently, during the heated discussions that preceded the establishment of the Central African Federation, the African Congress leaders called on the Churches to hold a Day of Prayer to ask God to prevent federation from coming to pass. The political implications of such a suggestion were obvious, and the great majority of the African ministers, with no prompting or persuasion from their European colleagues, came to the conclusion that the Church should not be committed in this way to one side in the dispute, even though great numbers of African Christians were then opposed to federation. So, instead of specifying in their public prayers what they personally hoped would be the outcome, they made the Day of Prayer an occasion of heart-searching for the Church, and called on their people to intercede on behalf of those upon whom the burden of decision was resting, that, with all the facts before them, they should be alert and open to the guidance of God's Spirit.

However, where there is an overwhelming conviction among Christian people that a certain course is the right one, it is good that public prayer should be offered for such a cause. So, for example, after a reasonable period for the proper weighing of the facts, the Churches in Buganda regularly offered prayers with one accord for the speedy return of the Kabaka during the period of his exile. Similarly, the Churches in the Gold Coast several times called the nation to prayer; notably during January 1956, when the country was 'threatened by internal dissension', and a call was made to 'men of goodwill of all parties to make it clear that they abhor and renounce all violence', in a 'Universal Week of Prayer'.

As has already been pointed out, African people have generally a very strong sense of the social and civil functions of religion; and although there are obvious dangers in an alliance which makes the Church merely the handmaid of the State, yet it is a very right feeling which expects the major undertakings of government to be supported by the prayers of the Church. In 1954 the Governments of both the Eastern and Western Regions of Nigeria asked for special services before the first session of the House of Assembly, and in each case one of the Anglican diocesan bishops preached. Again, the Minister of Education for the Western Region asked for special prayers in all the Churches on the Sunday prior to the new Education Act taking effect in January 1955, and there were special services with this intention throughout the Western Region. The Minister's letter making this request ran as follows:

The Regional Government in launching this immense programme of a magnitude never before attempted in Nigeria, humbly recognize that they have committed themselves to the compassion of Almighty God without whose merciful assistance and guidance, success cannot be achieved. . . . In particular we are asking you to pray for the teachers who will teach these children that they may be dedicated to the service of youth and to the great task which is before them.

Those who knew the people concerned recognized that there was no cant in this appeal; it was a true demonstration that the government was sensible of the responsibility which the Christian Church must bear towards it.

The proper fulfilment of this task, however, demands that the Church's regular worship shall contain intercessions in a form of words relevant to its present situation. Those Churches which make use of the Anglican Book of Common Prayer or similar ancient orders of service have a rich heritage for which to be thankful. But the bald translation into an African vernacular of a seventeenth-century prayer book is a most inadequate vehicle for the Church's expression of its intercession in the mid-twentieth century; and the African tendency to stick rigidly to the prescribed form has meant that other collections of prayers, such as are common in Great Britain, are very little used. There is no doubt that this has seriously deepened the impression that the Church is not interested in the contemporary affairs of men. Nothing short of bold revision of, and addition to, the authorized prayer books, will succeed in bringing realism and relevance into the intercession of the African Church.

(2) The Church as a whole is called to act as a leaven in society. A worshipping, disciplined community, dedicated to Christ's way and honestly attempting to realize His standards in its corporate life, is bound to affect the whole climate of the people among whom it is placed. The Church can serve the State best by illustrating in its own life the kind

of life which is God's will for society as a whole. Only then will it be in a position to rebuke the State for its sins and failures, for which both individual Christians, and the Church as a body, must acknowledge their own share of responsibility.

We have touched here upon one of the most painful problems which the Church has to face afresh in each generation with regard to its own life. The Church must be rooted in the society within which it has grown up. Its members are a part of that society, sharing its traditional points of view, influenced by its past history, and involved in its strength and its weakness, its rise or fall. A Church which is cut off from the rest of society, living a separate, enclosed life of its own, will be ineffectual; and will probably, in the end, become paralysed or perish altogether. And yet, at the same time, the Church must over and over again oppose and repudiate the attitudes and the standards which are accepted in the rest of society, otherwise it ceases to be the Christian Church.

When the rest of society is carried away on the waves of nationalist emotion, the Christians have to temper their nationalism with certain reservations and wider loyalties. This is equally true of a European country in time of war, of an African country in its struggle for political independence, or of an Asian country in the revival of its ancient culture. Or again, when the people as a whole accept the customary attitudes towards such things as marriage and divorce, or a system of caste, or the use of *lobola* (wrongly called 'the bride-price'), the Church must question and rethink all such customs in the light of its own Gospel. The Christian community is always reluctant to become too different from the rest of society, lest it appear as something alien and out of touch; and yet if the Church fails to give a reforming example that is consistent with its preaching, it becomes as salt which has lost its savour. A former Vice-Principal of St Paul's College, Calcutta, has pointed out that

thoughtful young people with a burning desire for justice will not listen to the Church's condemnation of Communism unless the Church's life matches her words and they can find in Christians

54

a real practice of community and a desire to 'undo the heavy burdens and let the oppressed go free . . . ' Alas, the ancient Syrian Church of Travancore has in fact been content for many centuries to occupy a position of privilege, closely equivalent to that of a highly placed Hindu caste. Christian landlords have virtually owned their outcaste serfs, and bought and sold them with the land, just like their Hindu neighbours. . . . Is it surprising that many young people have ceased to look to the Church for leadership in the fight against want, ignorance, and bondage, and have turned to the Communists?[1]

The Church can and must set its own house in order. It cannot avoid being involved in the economic and social life of the community; but as the 1937 Oxford Conference stressed:

In regard to the sources of income, methods of raising money, and administration of property, as well as in the terms on which it employs men and women and their tenure of office, Churches ought to be scrupulous to avoid the evil that Christians deplore in secular society.[2]

In those societies in Africa which are divided by race or colour the Church must demonstrate real unity in its own minority society. Christians should be prepared to recognize with more open-hearted contrition, without trying to rationalize or excuse themselves, that they have been involved in forms of economic injustice and racial discrimination which make it impossible for the Church to appear, as it should, as the agent of that profound revolution in the hearts of men which is called the Kingdom of God. Every Christian community should face realistically the practical measures that are needed to diminish and eliminate all such division and unfairness within its own membership.

The witness of Christ's Church throughout Africa is terribly crippled by the refusal of a certain number of white Christians to accept non-Europeans into their homes, or even into their Churches, and by their silent acquiescence in

1. C. S. Milford, *India Revisited* (Highway Press, 1953), p. 35.
2. *The Churches Survey Their Task*, p. 126.

policies that are dictated by race-prejudice. Many Europeans can bear testimony to the pastoral ministrations which they received during their military service from African army chaplains; and yet a few years ago, when the Bishop of Mashonaland said that Europeans must be prepared to accept the Sacrament at the hands of African priests, the suggestion brought an outcry from certain elements in the Church.

Fortunately the Church's record in this respect has not been entirely lamentable. Christian Missions have pioneered the way of equal partnership, and their institutions have been the first in many parts of Africa to appoint African principals with authority over European staff. Thousands of white Christians are waging an honest fight against the unconscious attitudes of superiority and condescension which persist so subtly in themselves, and the Church as a whole is steadily putting its own house in order in this respect.

The Anglican Cathedral, Nairobi, which until a few years ago was entirely 'white' in practice, though never by precept, has now a definitely multi-racial congregation, and an African minister serves on the Cathedral staff. In Abercorn, in Northern Rhodesia, a Church has recently been founded which, instead of being the usual European chaplaincy Church, is quite definitely regarded as an 'English-speaking' Church to which African, Indian, and European Christians will be equally welcome. A new Church has recently been built at the Kilembe copper mine in Western Uganda, where white South African and Rhodesian mining technicians have for three years been pastorally in the sole care of a young African priest. Under his inspiration the Church was planned, and during the last stages of its construction Africans, Canadians, white South Africans, and English laboured side by side to finish the work in time for the dedication ceremony, at which those who had worked as one now worshipped as one, and will continue to do so as far as language differences permit.

There is no room for complacency, and the Church must never be satisfied until it can exhibit to the world a community in which all trace of division has been purged away. But the witness is being given with steadily increasing positiveness and consistency. The Provincial Synod of the Anglican Church in South Africa at its session in 1950 called on all members of the Church to examine their racial attitudes, 'that in every parish witness may be borne to the equal standing of all Churchmen before God and to their brotherhood one with another in Christ'. In this way it drew attention to the crux of the matter, namely, that whatever pronouncements the official organs of the Churches may make, the real point of Christian obedience is at the parish level, where the local Church community has to determine just how honestly Christian it is prepared to be. There is not much doubt that if distinctions based upon mere race and colour could be wholly eliminated from the Church, even though it is only a minority Church, the change would spread to the whole of society. It is the solemn responsibility of every Christian, be he black or white, to ask himself how sincerely he wants to see that happen.

(3) The Church as an institution has a particular responsibility to provide a meeting ground whereon Christians who belong to opposed parties and points of view may come together in mutual trust and frankness, on the basis of their common membership in Christ, to thrash out the problems that divide men and to reach a more sympathetic understanding of one another's thought. It may seem presumptuous for the Church to claim this responsibility when its own lack of unity is such a public scandal. And yet it is a hard fact that the disputants in political or industrial or international affairs very rarely confront one another except on a pitch that is already queered by prejudice, by lobbying, by press campaigns, or above all by personal maladjustment; and that quite often, when they are awake to their opportunities, the Churches can provide that forum for honest discussion and hard thinking wherein the inhibitions caused by bias or bitterness may be broken down in that new dimension which it is the Church's task to make real.

This sort of thing is taking place quietly and effectively in many parts of Africa. An excellent example is the Namirembe group, consisting mainly of young African professional men and their wives, with a smaller number of Europeans, which has been meeting weekly in the house of the Anglican bishop in Kampala for discussion, debate, or social recreation. During the exile of the Kabaka members of the delegation which had been in England to plead for his return came naturally to that group to report; and when the Governor, Sir Andrew Cohen, asked if he might attend to hear what was being said, the members of the group readily agreed on condition that he came as a private individual. It was a tribute to the atmosphere of honesty and sympathy generated by that group that the Buganda Lukiiko chose the bishop's conference room as the site for the deliberation of their representatives with Sir Keith Hancock later in the year, and called it 'the Namirembe Conference'.

An American missionary worker has emphasized both the profound difficulty of this task of understanding and reconciliation, and also the special calling of the Church in Africa to perform it:

The most important function of the missionary in Africa is that of establishing ties of intimate personal friendship with a certain number – necessarily small – of Africans. The formal intercourse of church, school, hospital or other professional relationships do not provide adequate channels for the deepest levels of communication. In fact the difficulty of true communication between people of different languages and cultures is seldom fully recognized . . . The only way to overcome this barrier is such prolonged and intimate fellowship that connotation both of idea, of feeling and of motive become shared, each one exploring deeply the other's mind and heart. If possible it should take place in the languages of both participants so that the conceptual resources of both languages may be freely utilized. It should, of course, not be merely abstract discussion but should be part of the experience of working together at whatever task is in hand. . . . Unquestionably it is by such sharing that the great spiritual pioneers and leaders of Africa have most often come to their full stature.[1]

1. Carpenter, *op. cit.*, p. 105.

Such debate, if it is to be fruitful in practical ways, demands not only the deep understanding of one another by the participants, but also an informed understanding of the issues which concern them. The social, economic, and political problems of Africa cannot be solved merely by goodwill alone. The discussion, for example, of the Dow Report on East Africa, or of the federal constitution of Nigeria, is shallow and futile unless it is enlightened by a good deal of expert knowledge. The relevant facts must be studied and mastered before any truthful judgement can be made. The Oxford Conference recommended that:

the Churches ought – when they are not already equipped for the purpose – to have at their service, regionally as well as oecumenically, organs both for study and research, as well as for witness and action in appropriate circumstances . . . In the past, pronouncements sometimes and preachings often have failed to carry weight because the speakers assumed a technical knowledge which they did not have. We would urge, therefore, that in the forming of Christian opinion there should be more co-operation between clergy and ministers, on the one hand, and those of the laity on the other, who are engaged in industry, commerce and public administration.[1]

It is easy to see how this should be applied by the Church in Africa, and there are numbers of Christian men and women – on the staffs of University Colleges, in the administration, in industry and commerce – who would gladly bring their specialized knowledge to aid the Church's honest wrestling with its task. The Christian Council of the Gold Coast has given a lead here; for example, it held a conference in May, 1955, attended by representatives from Nigeria and Liberia, as well as by lay Christian teachers, journalists, lawyers, lecturers, and welfare workers in the Gold Coast, to consider the important problem of African customs and their relation to the Christian faith.[2]

(4) It is not always understood that a very great deal of the social and political witness of the Christian Church is

1. *The Churches Survey Their Task*, p. 127.
2. See their Report: *Christianity and African Culture* (Accra, 1956).

made through the personal action of the official leaders of the Churches. Not infrequently the critics of the Church in Africa have complained that the Church has remained silent, when in fact some accredited leader and spokesman of the Church has achieved far more by private interview or correspondence than could ever have been achieved through some synodical pronouncement. It is known, for example, that during the developments of the past six years which have led Nigeria to the threshold of self-government, the African bishops have several times made representations to the leaders of the political parties; and that their Christian counsel was the more readily heeded because they were Africans and in sympathy with the nationalist cause.

The great Bishop Michael Furse, when he was about to leave South Africa in 1920, wrote a very long 'open letter' to General Smuts, setting out some of the grievances of the Bantu people and making three quite practical proposals that should lead to greater justice. At the next session of Parliament in Cape Town, new legislation was introduced on the lines of two of these suggestions, and the third was adopted later. Unfortunately the present Government of the Union has repealed all these Acts of Parliament.[1]

Another outstanding bishop in Africa, Frank Weston of Zanzibar, used on several occasions the weapon of the pamphlet in his capacity as bishop. During the 1914–18 war he published an Open Letter which was widely read, entitled *Black Slaves of Prussia*. He had had long experience of German administration in what was then German East Africa, and his plea was that the country should not be returned to Germany after the war. The pamphlet certainly influenced the decision to make it a mandated territory under Britain. In the early years of British administration, however, the bishop published another critical pamphlet, which he called *Serfs of Great Britain*! There is little doubt that the publicity given to this led to changes and a more enlightened policy.[2]

1. See Michael Furse, *Stand Therefore* (S.P.C.K., 1953), pp. 95–101.
2. See Maynard Smith, *Frank, Bishop of Zanzibar* (S.P.C.K., 1926), pp. 202 ff. and 240 ff.

Political Action by the Church

The autobiography of Bishop Furse describes another occasion when he was able to influence policy, this time in an industrial matter. Trouble arose from the custom which prevailed in most of the Johannesburg mines, and on the railways, of postponing until Sunday the repairs to machinery necessitated during the week, with the consequence that a large number of men never had a day off in the week. Those of the clergy who were in closest touch with the miners agreed that something ought to be done about it. Bishop Furse therefore consulted the heads of the various Christian denominations, including the Roman Catholic bishop. The result was a conference at which, having gone carefully into the whole business, and being sure of their facts, they drew up a statement to present to the Chamber of Mines and to the government. The Roman bishop did not see his way to take part in the conference, but he did sign the statement. After considerable delay they were granted an interview with a committee of the Chamber of Mines. The ultimate result was that the government passed legislation providing for one day off a week for all employees in the mines and on the railways.[1]

This quotation illustrates the kind of care which such a procedure requires. It also indicates the strength which is added to one man's appeal when he is able to combine with the heads of other denominations. A similar course, which is becoming increasingly common, was taken more recently by the leaders of the Christian Churches in Kenya, when on 4 December 1953 they published in the East African press their open letter on 'abuses of power by certain members of the forces of law and order'.

Apart from the greater numerical weight of such joint representations, the process of consultation which must necessarily precede any combined statement serves to disarm the opposition, who might otherwise argue that the opinion of a bishop is no more responsible or representative than that of any individual. Father Huddleston has described the failure of protests by individual Churches in South Africa

1. See Furse, *op. cit.*, p. 66.

61

against the 1954 Bantu Education Act, which was opposed by every Church authority in the country, except the Dutch Reformed Church:

The Minister was approached directly and indirectly by the different Churches and urged to reconsider his decisions. The tragic mistake, as I shall always believe, lay in the failure of the Churches to act together. I am convinced that had, say, the Methodists, the Roman Catholics, the Presbyterians and the Anglicans united for once on this single issue . . . at least some major concessions would have been won.[1]

Members of the Churches themselves also need to remember that if they wish the statements of their official leaders to command respect in high places they must not expect these men to rush as lightly or as frequently into public self-expression as others, who are no more than individual Christians, are able to do. It is futile and tragic when the 'voice of the Church', as represented by some high dignitary, can be quoted by both sides to support their own case, as happened in Central Africa during the federation controversy.

(5) Lastly we come to the use of resolutions and pronouncements by Church conferences, synods, and other religious assemblies. The value of these is two-edged. They serve to educate the members of the Church themselves, making them more aware of the ethical standards implied in their faith, and supporting with authority those ministers who are facing criticism and opposition in their efforts to interpret those standards to their people. They also exert a real influence on the policy of the State, not so much by a direct effect upon the government as by moulding public opinion. It is in these terms that we must judge the value of the long series of statements made in South Africa over the past eight years by the Episcopal, Provincial, and Diocesan Synods of the Anglican Church, and by the highest councils of other Churches, concerning racialism in its various aspects.

There are, however, such grave dangers in too great reliance on this method, which appeals so strongly to many

1. T. Huddleston, *Naught For Your Comfort* (Collins, 1956), p. 171.

Christians, that it is worth quoting at length some of the warnings issued on this subject in 1937 by Dr J. H. Oldham:

> The practice of passing resolutions and making pronouncements is beset with dangers and may often be a sheer waste of time. . . . Reliance on mistaken or futile methods of procedure cannot but weaken the influence of the Church for good. . . . Pronouncements which do not have behind them a solid body of considered and convinced opinion can have little or no effect on public action. Astute politicians and experienced civil servants are quite capable of assessing the amount of real force which lies behind such resolutions, and of attaching to them the weight that they deserve. . . . Secondly the habit of passing resolutions, carried to excess, defeats its own purpose. Where opinions are easily, cheaply, and glibly expressed they are accorded little public attention. . . . Finally we have to take account of the immense amount of valuable time that might be expended much more fruitfully in other directions which is often spent in the passing and debating of resolutions . . . Christian assemblies must not allow themselves to become involved in futilities of this kind if the influence of the Church is to count in a world in which there are movements which are in deadly earnest.[1]

If public statements by the official organs of the Church are to carry weight, therefore, they must be disinterested, united, and severely practical.

(a) *Disinterested.* From time to time the Church as a body must fight for the rights of its individual members. For example, when a Sharia court in Egypt annulled the marriage of a Moslem girl convert with a Christian man, it was the Christian community which fought the case in a special court of the Ministry of Justice and obtained a reversal of the decision.[2] But whenever the Church's protests begin to look like self-interest, even when that is not strictly the case (as in her fight for religious liberties), it is of the utmost importance that such suspicions should be dispelled by an exhibition of equal concern for all underprivileged people of whatever faith. When that great Christian, Dr H. C.

1. Visser t'Hooft and J. H. Oldham, *The Church and Its Function in Society* (Allen & Unwin, 1937), pp. 223–5.
2. See *International Review of Missions*, October, 1933.

Mukerjee, a member of the Bengal legislature and of the constituent assembly which drafted the constitution, maintained the view that Christians should not ask for the safeguard of special electorates which the British government had given, this was regarded by Nehru and others as an important contribution to building that consciously non-communal sense of citizenship which is one of India's greatest needs.[1]

(b) *United*. We have already seen the greater value of joint action between the leaders of various Christian bodies, and the weakness inherent in any statement which is not genuinely representative of the convictions of the Church. Herein lies the peculiar value of oecumenical organization, that is to say, united thought and action by different branches of the world-wide Church. This makes it possible for representatives of many denominations to reach a common Christian mind on social and political issues. At the highest level, the Commission of the Churches on International Affairs is able to hold a watching brief in the United Nations Organization on behalf of the Christian Church, and to make representations to international conferences and organizations, as, for example, in the communication which was delivered to the four Foreign Ministers when they met in Berlin in February 1954. At the regional level, the same sort of thing can now be done through local Christian Councils. In all these joint organizations there is always the danger of their agreed statements becoming so vague and generalized as to be of no practical value. Many Christians in Central Africa, for example, felt that the agreed statement on the federation question issued by the Christian Council, having taken into account all the shades of opinion from the different Missions and Churches represented, was so innocuous as to be meaningless for action.

(c) *Practical*. In drawing up such resolutions the members of the assemblies would do well to ask themselves: exactly *who* is hereby committing himself to do precisely *what?* If the

1. See Milford, *op. cit.*, p. 12.

answer is in doubt it may be assumed that the resolution is not worth passing. It is certain that if this standard had been set, a great many of the wordy statements which have issued from religious assemblies in all parts of Africa would never have been made. It is this consideration for positive action which should serve as a caution to those who pin their faith to protests made on African affairs by Christian bodies in Britain or elsewhere. Where the issues are ultimately the concern of the British voter, it is clearly a perfectly practical step to attempt to influence public opinion. But on the other issues, such as the *apartheid* policy of the Nationalist Government of South Africa, Christians in Britain can do no good by meeting merely for the purpose of making irresponsible noises of anger and dismay. Statements, if they are made at all, must be accurate, responsible, and helpful, thought out on the basis of Dr Edgar Brookes' wise saying:

The difficulties of South Africa are the world's difficulties on a smaller scale; and we should meet them together rather than as the superior critic and the exasperated subject of criticism.

To recapitulate the fivefold action which the Church as a corporate body may take in the social and political field: this consists of its prayer, the example of its own community, the provision of a place of meeting for discussion and understanding, the personal intervention of its leaders, and official pronouncements and resolutions. If the Church in Africa is to fulfil this many-sided task effectively it must be the real Church of the people, and not a 'Mission' or 'colonial' Church. Its roots must be in Africa and not outside. It must welcome black, white, and brown Christians into equal membership, and that welcome must be accepted and valued equally by all. Until that happens the Church will always be partial, divided, crippled in its witness.

Some years ago a political prisoner in Lagos prison said to the African chaplain, 'Don't come and talk to me, until your Church, after its hundred years of existence, can show an African Diocesan Bishop. We are tired of always being assistants.' That is remedied now in Nigeria; but what of the other territories?

The Presbyterian Church in Nyasaland has been, in recent years, growing more aware of the need for full integration of Church and Mission, so that responsibility for decision on major matters should more and more reside locally and not require reference overseas, while the representatives of the sending Church should become fully members and ministers of the Church now established in Nyasaland. A correspondent from that Church has written:

We must have a Church so organized that it is shown to be a home for all races. In the system that I know best, we must not have work among Europeans linked to Scotland, and work among Africans confined to Church courts for Africans, but rather achieve a unity even in organization.

Some branches of the Church in Africa have already gone much further along that way; others are still bogged down in sectional organization. It is certain that only a Church which has paid the price of unity, and can demonstrate it in its organization as well as in its ideals, can either think straight or talk straight about politics in Africa.

CHAPTER FIVE

Differences of Opinion

'I BESEECH you in the bowels of Christ, think it possible you may be mistaken.' These well-known words were written by Oliver Cromwell in 1650 in a letter to the General Assembly of the Church of Scotland, whom, though he was fighting them on a political issue, he regarded as his fellow Christians. The words might well be remembered by all who are profoundly convinced that their cause is just and their point of view the right one. For the real heart of democracy lies in the necessity for every leader and every party to 'think it possible that they may be mistaken', and to recognize the sincerity and integrity of their opponents. In public affairs, therefore, it is most necessary to cultivate the tolerance of Voltaire, who said 'I disapprove of what you say, but I will defend to the death your right to say it.'

This is something which needs to be better understood in Africa, where there is often great bewilderment because Christians do not all hold the same opinions on practical issues. Many people tend to think, with a simple directness, that in any question one answer must be true and all others false, that in any situation one line of behaviour is correct and all others wrong, and that if people will not say clearly which is the right way then they must either be too stupid to see it or too hypocritical to admit it.

This attitude is often extended to Christian principles. Surely, it is argued, all Christians must agree on the basic principles of their faith, and if a policy is opposed to such principles, then all Christians must condemn it. So also the Christian's task in the political field is to apply the principles of Christianity to the social and economic problems of his people, and, where that is done, all Christians must surely support it. Such a proposition sounds reasonable enough, and it is said that one cause of African bewilderment and disillusionment with the Church is that they feel it is not facing honestly the problems of principle which are involved in Africa to-day.

The word 'principle' is one of those vague terms which have a strange power of appealing to the emotions while conveying extremely little to the intelligence. Ordinarily sensible men excuse their most childish quarrels by saying that a matter of principle is at stake. We are dealing, therefore, with one of those dangerously dynamic words which Christians ought only to handle with the utmost care and the most scrupulous honesty.

We have to admit in the first place that 'principles' are often quoted to give a cloak of respectability to parties or individuals, when in fact there is no content whatever in the words that are used. The great Dr Johnson once said of an acquaintance of his, 'I am afraid he has not been in the inside of a Church for many years, but he never passes a Church without pulling off his hat. This shows that he has good principles.' There are some people in Africa who will raise their hat, as it were, to the principles of 'partnership' or 'non-discrimination', yet in practice these words commit them to absolutely nothing at all. And when Christian principles are turned into party slogans these also may mean as much or as little as is convenient for the people concerned. There is a dangerous futility in the rather pompous codification of principles and 'rights of man' by global councils such as U.N.O., dangerous because it can so easily lead on to disillusionment and despair.

Then we must also face the fact that principles may be invoked to support almost any action. There are members of the Dutch Reformed Church who quote 'Christian principles' in support of a policy of *apartheid* and their programme of 'Christian National Education', as sincerely as Father Huddleston has quoted them in opposition to it. There are white Kenyans who believe that the Federal Independence Party offers the best hope of preserving 'Christian values' in East Africa, while their opponents are working for a genuinely multi-racial government also on the grounds of Christian

68

principles. Bernard Shaw with mocking shrewdness said in *The Man of Destiny*:

There is nothing so bad or so good that you will not find Englishmen doing it; but you will never find an Englishman in the wrong. He does everything on principle. He fights you on patriotic principles; he robs you on business principles; he enslaves you on imperial principles.

When people talk about principles they are often trying to take a short cut which avoids the necessity of what William Blake called 'mental fight'. For the real problem does not generally lie in the principle (which is usually a truth which is not much in dispute anyway) but in its application. It is there that the disagreement arises, and the reaffirmation of the principle does nothing to reconcile the divided parties. As Dr Johnson said about the opposing political parties of his day: 'Their principles are the same though their modes of thinking are different.' Nothing can eliminate the necessity for deep and prolonged thinking about the problems of application, and Christians should not be guilty of that theoretical over-simplification of the issues which betrays a flippant attitude to the truth. Dr Oldham has written of this humble and hardworking approach to the problems of society:

Nothing is more irritating to those engaged in politics, administration and industry, who know the intractability of the problems with which they are wrestling, than the suggestion that the parson, as parson, has the answers all the time in his pocket, or what is practically the same thing, that all that is necessary is to 'apply Christian principles' . . . To bring about effective Christian action in modern society with its many perplexities a new development is needed in the life of the Church – the formation on a large scale of groups of lay men and women who will meet, not to discuss the abstract principles of Christian ethics, but to take counsel together about the concrete decisions which they have to make in their daily occupations and to fortify one another in making them.[1]

This immediate wrestling with the problems in hand is, of course, the daily business of politics. The opposition may

1. J. H. Oldham, *Life is Commitment* (S.C.M., 1953), pp. 86 and 107.

invoke an abstract principle in its attack on the government; politicians may offer a cut and dried programme in their election campaigns; but the government in power has to make its immediate political decisions in relation to a given concrete situation which, because it is always unique, no theory can ever fit precisely. There has to be adaptation and compromise; the demands of a variety of interests have to be satisfied as far as possible in a balanced way; and use must be made of the factors available at the time. A month later the situation has changed, and so the methods of dealing with it must likewise be different. As Disraeli said, 'Finality is not the language of politics.'

So far from disconcerting the Christian, this state of affairs should rather appeal to him, for what is, of necessity, the politician's way of doing the best thing is also the Biblical way of obeying the will of God. The practice of formulating ethical principles and then setting out to apply them to the realities of life has nothing in common with the spirit of the Bible. It was the Greeks who believed that there was a grand, universal law which rules the universe, and that it was men's duty to discover and apply this law of goodness to individual human life and society, and to bring the human race nearer towards the fixed ideal. But the Bible view of life does not present us with any fixed ideal or any norm of right behaviour. Men are required not to obey a code of laws but to answer the call of the living God as it comes to them through the ever new demands of each concrete situation.

God did not speak once for all. His Will for His people was clarified in certain particular directions from time to time by Moses and by later teachers, as the changing situation of the Hebrew people presented them with fresh decisions in new circumstances. The prophets, in later generations, did not quote the ancient laws nor attempt to deduce from them certain underlying principles, but they called the people to an immediate personal response to the God of the present moment: 'Thus saith the Lord . . .' 'To-day if ye will hear His voice harden not your hearts.' And Jesus Christ supremely maintained that the greater righteousness was not the follow-

ing of all the laws which men, through their dread of freedom, had tried to codify and fix, but a direct personal
obedience, moment by moment, to the call of the Heavenly
Father. If men know God they will begin to know His Will,
but they will only know it as His call comes to them through
the demands of the here and now which confronts them.
Dietrich Bonhoeffer, who as a Christian pastor played his
part in politics so positively that he was hanged by the Nazis
in Germany, wrote from his prison in Berlin:

Who stands his ground? Only the man whose ultimate criterion is
not in his reason, his principles, his conscience, his freedom or his
virtue, but who is ready to sacrifice all these things when he is
called to obedient and responsible action in faith and exclusive
allegiance to God. The responsible man seeks to make his whole
life a response to the question and call of God.[1]

Dr Oldham has also pointed out that:

The task of the Christian is not to lay down abstract principles to
which life must conform, but to fight evil where he encounters it;
and since evil can entrench itself in social and political institutions
it has to be resisted and overcome there as well as in the life of the
individual.[2]

If men are seeking to know God and His will, and to hear
His call in the world of to-day, they must realize that in this
pattern of experience there are two elements which are
capable of change. Men's knowledge of God will deepen and
develop, particularly as they wrestle with the problems of
obedience to His will through debate and by experiment.
Then again the situation here and now will continually be
changing, so presenting a different demand to be obeyed.
We can see sometimes one, sometimes another, of these two
elements of change in the attempt by Christians to understand the meaning of righteousness and justice in their
contemporary situation.

For example, for very many centuries Christians have

1. Dietrich Bonhoeffer, *Letters and Papers from Prison* (S.C.M., 1953),
p. 15.
2. Oldham, *op. cit.*, p. 101.

known God as the Lord of justice and of mercy. And yet they do not seem to have felt until quite recently that slavery, the subjection of women, the burning of heretics, or the use of torture were fundamentally contrary to God's will, though here and there a few isolated individuals made their protest. It was a remarkable change in the whole pattern of European thinking, sometimes called the Enlightenment, which brought the Church also to greater sensitiveness towards the will of God in these respects.

This deeper understanding has never come suddenly to the whole Church at once. One or two men of vision begin to suspect that the traditional view has not been close enough to the true will of God. Their first attempts at change are met with misunderstanding and opposition; long discussion and controversy follows; out of the clash of argument between Christian and Christian emerges a new insight which captures the imagination and the obedience of a great part of the Church. Often that Christian minority – but not always – is the first element in society to develop new attitudes with regard to a particular issue, and so, acting as the conscience of society, to bring about reform and advance.

This can be seen in the story of the development of public opinion concerning slavery. From time immemorial there have been slaves in every civilized society. Reformers sought to mitigate its cruelties, but it never occurred to them that slavery itself could be eliminated. The Roman master had complete rights of life and limb over his slaves; in that world the Hebrew Scriptures were almost unique in that they included slaves under the protection of the law, which also forbade Jews to sell their own people into slavery, or to keep those that had sold themselves for longer than seven years. The Church also accepted slavery as an inevitable institution; its great contribution in the early centuries was that it welcomed slaves as men of equal dignity in God's eyes. 'Among us,' wrote Ignatius in the second century, 'there is no difference between slaves and masters, nor any reason why we share the name of brethren except that we believe ourselves to be equal.'

72

Differences of Opinion

Slowly this rather shocking attitude had its effect upon public opinion, and the laws began to extend certain rights to the slave population. Though the Churches, when they became property owners, kept their own slaves, they set an example of mercy and fellowship in their dealings with them. Following the example of the Jewish law, Christians then condemned the sale of other Christians; but by a strange and tragic blindness they failed to see that this prohibition must extend equally to the enslavement of any men, and their failure finally to slam the door against all slavery made possible the dreadful resurgence of the negro slave trade at the beginning of the modern era.

However, individual Christians were beginning to sense that slavery as such was an evil thing. Ambrose, and many pious leaders after him, used both their own and the Church's wealth to buy slaves in order to set them free. Pope Gregory the Great at the end of the sixth century was the first to give slaves their freedom on the grounds that all men are equal. A century later an Abbot in Constantinople left in his will an order that no monastery might ever again own slaves, saying: 'the slave no less than the free man is made in the image of God'. Sweden has the honour of being the first nation, in the thirteenth century, to pass a law forbidding without exception the sale of human beings.

Meanwhile, for various historical and economic reasons, the ownership and sale of slaves as personal property fell into disuse, and was superseded by the ownership and sale of estates with the labourers, who were attached to the soil, included in the property. So the slaves were replaced by the serfs. The Middle Ages saw their gradual enfranchisement and the appearance of the paid labourer. By the fifteenth century Christendom had almost succeeded in achieving a universal freedom, when suddenly Africa and America fell open to the new merchants of Europe and their heartless lust for gain opened a new chapter in the story of slavery.

Even in those dark days some Christian voices were raised against the inhuman exploitation, first of the natives of the West Indies, then, as they were decimated, of the West

73

Africans who were shipped to replace them. Las Casas, who until his ninety-second year battled for justice and humanity, and others of the Dominicans, together with Isabella the Queen of Spain, stood out against slavery; but they went down before the tide of greed. Soon the traffic in slaves offered as great rewards as even the mines and estates of the New World, and England, to her shame, won the monopoly of the slave trade. But through all this darkness of degradation the Church was almost never without some voice to keep conscience alive. George Fox and, after him, other Quakers, were among the pioneers. Richard Baxter, the Presbyterian, condemned all who engaged in the trade as 'fitter to be called incarnate devils than Christians'. In the eighteenth century John Woolman the Quaker and Benjamin Franklin, in America, and Granville Sharp, the amateur lawyer in Britain, were the forerunners of that little army of Christian champions who flung the final challenge to the grim giant of slavery that had spoiled the face of the earth for so many centuries.

The last fight was desperate. Many Christians, blindly though sincerely misapplying the very Scriptures which to-day are quoted in support of racialism, were opposed to the reforms. But out of the controversy the truth emerged with ever-growing clarity. Albert Barnes prophesied in America in 1846: 'The defence of slavery from the Bible is to be and will soon be abandoned and men will wonder that any defence of such a system could have been attempted from the Word of God.' So at last, from the faithful witness of the few, the conscience of the whole Church was stung wide awake and roused the peoples of many nations to bring this ancient evil to an end. Only in the final stage of the struggle did the Church speak with a single voice; and yet through all the centuries it was from within the Church that the disturbing, challenging ideas emerged; it was in the unfolding life of the Christian community that men discovered, generation after generation, one more step forward in obedience to the call of God.

For this life, as Dr Oldham has stressed, 'has to be lived

without Christian programmes . . . The only programme for
the Christian is to obey God in the situation in which he has
been placed.'[1] But that situation, as we have seen, is constantly subject to change, and thereby introduces a new
emphasis or a fresh understanding in the Christian's idea of
what is the right thing to do. An example of this is found in
the Church's attitude towards poverty. Leaving on one side
those members of the Church who have been callously
blind or indifferent to the needs of the poor, we can see how
new economic circumstances have in fact changed the thinking of the truly responsible Christians as to what is the call of
God to them in the matter. For many centuries a poverty
which deprived a part of society of the physical necessities of
life was an inevitable factor in the very constitution of the
economic order. The very best minds could see it only as a
permanent feature of every human society. 'The poor ye
have always with you.' Christian obedience to God in that
sort of society meant costly charity; for some shining individuals there was even a call to abandon all privilege and
share to the utmost the lot of the abject poor.

But, as a result of great social change and the enormous
development of economic techniques, the abolition of such
poverty now seems to be within man's control through his
organization of economic life. This possibility of economic
plenty marks off our age from early periods in which Christian
thinking about poverty was formulated. Now not individual
paupers, but the persistence of poverty itself has become a
matter for which men are morally responsible. In the light
of this fact, Christian obedience to God means the devotion
of life and effort not towards paternal charity but towards the
realization of a more just distribution of the world's wealth
amongst all the peoples of the world.

If Christian ethics, then, are always relative and progressive; if Christian obligation must always be experienced as a
direct personal response to God's call in the here and now,
are we to conclude that there are no principles, no fixed
standards, by which to judge of a nation's righteousness or

1. Oldham, *op. cit.*, p. 101.

an individual's morality? In one sense that is true, and it is this insight which underlies Christ's own profound injunction, 'Judge not'. But though the idea of fixed Christian principles is one we would do well to abandon, there remains our knowledge of God as revealed in Jesus Christ; and from that deepening personal encounter with Him we derive certain convictions about His will for man and man's life, which remain unalterable however much we may go on discovering about the practical means of obeying His will in any particular situation.

As we seek to discern that will in any particular set of circumstances we do not approach the matter with vacant minds. Out of the Bible and in the Church we are receiving all the time a deepening knowledge of God and a growing understanding of his purpose and his methods. We do not use the Bible as a 'book of words' which tells us what to do in any emergency, but we submit to it as *the* Word. That is to say, we allow the Bible as a whole – its record of the acts of God and its inspired interpretation of them, all culminating in the supreme Act, when the Word was made flesh, suffered and died, rose again and ascended – so to dominate and shape our thinking, judging, and feeling that we become more and more intensely aware of the character of God and of His impact upon us. Out of the Bible and in the Church God comes, as it were, striding to meet us in our contemporary situation; and in that meeting we find an absolute demand to do His will in His way, and a devouring conviction as to what that will and that way really are.'

It is enormously important, however, that we defend and proclaim these convictions, not as moral principles, self-evident and self-contained, but as insights into truth resulting from our personal encounter with, and faith in, a particular kind of God. Moreover, since that encounter calls, not for an ethical pronouncement but for an immediate obedience, Christians will not rest on any generalization, but must strive to work out at once, in the given situation, the implications of their understanding of God.

Dr Oldham has shown that the Gospel is not itself a law,

and that the individual must bear the responsibility of decision in each particular situation:

> To give him precise instructions to be literally carried out is to rob him of his moral responsibility as a person . . . Hence between purely general statements of the ethical demands of the Gospel and the decisions that have to be made in concrete situations, there is need for what may be described as middle axioms. It is these that give relevance and point to the Christian ethic. They are not binding for all time but are provisional definitions of the type of behaviour required of Christians at a given period and in given circumstances.[1]

Christian thought, therefore, should move from the direct knowledge of the nature of God to proposals for action within the social and political sphere. First, the basis of Christian concern in the economic order must be seen to lie in the Church's understanding of God and of His purpose to restore men's lost dignity and worth. Secondly, this understanding of the purpose of God may be seen to throw a searchlight on the actual facts of the existing situation; and a critical analysis of the present economic order, for example, will show up many points at which it must be challenged by Christian understanding of life. And so, thirdly, comes the place for those 'middle axioms' related to given circumstances. It is this process which saves statements of principles from being platitudes, and which makes possible practical Christian decisions leading to action. At this point, of course, differences of opinion often arise. Some Christians, for example, believe that the economic order can best be made to accord with the divine purpose for man within the framework of a system of private enterprise; other Christians demand a different system, primarily based upon the social ownership of the means of production.

We must recognize that such differences are partly differences of judgement which honest minds face in any realm of human decision; but they are also partly caused by the partiality, due to historical or economic factors, which

1. W. A. Visser t'Hooft and J. H. Oldham, *op. cit.*, p. 209.

mars all human choice. The Oxford Conference of 1937 made a very important pronouncement in this connexion:

The Christian Church is a fellowship in Christ which transcends differences of judgement and divergences of action in relation to the concrete economic situation. Further, if only Christians are brought to repentance in the light of the Christian message they can never maintain that attitude of fanatical hatred towards members of other groups which is now so common in the world. They and their opponents are both sinners in the presence of God, and the recognition of this fact, in social as well as in personal terms, would itself be a great constructive contribution towards moderating the bitterness of the struggle between social groups.[1]

These three stages of thought, which might be defined as theological, critical, and practical, should be applied by Christians in Africa to all the burning issues of that continent. The claptrap of propaganda slogans must be ignored. Profound Christian convictions about the nature of God and his design for mankind must throw their searchlight upon the evils of racial tension, upon the claims of African nationalism, upon the economic needs of African countries, and upon the constitutional problems of the so-called 'multi-racial societies'. Thus far, then, Christians should expect to be able to reach a common mind; but in the *practical* proposals which result from this approach they must be prepared to find deep differences of opinion amongst themselves.

There is no simple answer to such dilemmas as the issue between federal or unitary constitutions in Uganda or the Gold Coast, the question whether, in Nigeria or Tanganyika, priority should be given to industrialization or to the large-scale development of co-operatives, or the choice between communal land tenure or wholesale private freehold. These deep divergences will be something for Christians to accept without rancour, because their fellowship and their trust in one another's integrity overarches and embraces them all; and also because they believe that, within an atmosphere of mutual respect, the clash of opposing views and the long

1. *The Churches Survey Their Task*, pp. 110–14.

wrestling of continuous debate may bring to birth a truer understanding of the way of obedience to God.

It is this truly Christian insight into the need for honest controversy which leads the Church in our own day to attach such value to democratic forms of government. 'Democracy', however, like 'principles', is an emotional word that is often used but rarely understood; Christians, therefore, particularly need to realize what it is and what it is not. Democratic government is not necessarily the only form of government of which a Christian can approve. The absolute power of one wise and good man may, in certain circumstances, be admirable; the government of one people by those of another nation may also, in certain circumstances, be the best possible; provided, in both cases, that the rulers have the consent of the people. But the more intelligently responsible the people become, the more they will need to express their consent in democratic forms. For the Christian, the real basis of democracy is the fact of human fallibility. Good government must provide for the possibility, nay, the certainty, of any ruler making a mistake; and democratic machinery does precisely that.

Again, the Christian can never subscribe to the statement which is often made in Africa as a justification of democracy, that the majority is always right. The reading of history – of the story of slavery for example, which we have just been recalling – will soon show that again and again the minority is right. Democracy is good, not because it expresses the opinion of the majority on each issue, but because it ensures that the government is in power by the consent of the majority. The members of a legislature are not there as delegates, though that is a very common fallacy; they are there as elected legislators. Their task is not to be a mouthpiece for someone else's opinions, but to legislate according to the best wisdom which they by the process of debate can devise. They have to do what is just, not what is popular. There is, therefore, a grave weakness in any sort of communal representation, whether the member is expected to speak for a trade union, or a racial community. The young man who said 'To-day I vote, not as an African, but as a Rhodesian' may have caused misgivings in the minds of his friends, but he had a true sense of politics. The parties forming a government should also stand for policies, and not for classes or races or other sectional interests. The grave weakness of any communal representation is that it perpetuates the self-concern of the minorities, instead of drawing them into the common interest in securing the ablest legislators and the soundest policies. Christians, therefore, cannot be satisfied with any aim less than the achievement of universal adult suffrage, on a common roll, in their territory. [1]

The fallacy that the majority must be right is something that the emergent political parties in all parts of British Africa have to guard against. One of the most harmful results of colonial government, as seen in those territories, lies in the way in which it inevitably gives birth to, and at the same time frustrates, the African urge towards independence, so that the desire for self-government dominates all African political planning to the exclusion of almost every other concern. An association which does not make African self-government its main objective stands little chance of popular support, and the various political groups tend to differ from one another only in the vehemence with which they are prepared to fight for it. This is a very poor preparation for ultimate political responsibility. It meant in West Africa, for example, that the Convention People's Party in the Gold Coast and the National Council of Nigeria and the Cameroons, when they first came into power on the flood tide of nationalism, found themselves in responsibility having

1. The achievement of a common roll in multi-racial societies must probably come about by a process of planned development from a system of communal representation as the first stage only, unless some system of indirect voting is adopted. Not only must minorities be safeguarded, but the mass of illiterate country folk must be protected from the exploitation to which mass propaganda can subject them if they are given a vote on national issues that are beyond their comprehension. This is certainly one of those questions of ways and means about which there can be no clear judgement of right and wrong and on which sincere Christians will hold opposing points of view.

more or less to work out their programme as they went along.

When no clearly defined political issues separate the parties, the Government seeks to bolster its strength by fanatical devotion to a powerful leader, while the opposition tends too easily to disintegrate into religious or tribal loyalties in default of any positive alternative programme of political action. This is no carping criticism; in the circumstances, no other outcome is possible. But there is an obvious need in each of the emergent African States for the appearance of at least two comprehensive parties, with a nation-wide appeal, diverging from each other on purely political rather than on sectional lines. It may be that the line of demarcation will be drawn as between the rural, chieftainly, conservative type of party (as represented by the National Liberation Movement in the Gold Coast, the Northern People's Congress of Nigeria, or James Miti's original Bataka Association in Uganda), and the new model radical type of party (as represented by the C.P.P. in the Gold Coast, the Action Group in Nigeria, and the Uganda National Congress).[1]

In the state of transition in some territories, when parties are formulating their doctrines, while in others African associations are only beginning to emerge, Christians have a supreme responsibility which on no account must they shirk.

---

1. The word 'party' is here used very loosely to cover a variety of political organizations. There are in fact three distinct degrees of development observable in political associations in Africa: (a) *The pressure group*, which seeks to influence, but not to control, government on behalf of some special interests, e.g. the Aborigines Rights Protection Society in the Gold Coast as early as 1897, the Uganda Farmers' African Union prior to 1949, or the (white) Kenya Electors' Union. (b) *The nationalist movement*, which may be organized to secure control over government, either by achieving uni-racial self-government, e.g. the C.P.P. in the Gold Coast in 1950, the Nyasaland National Congress, and the (white) Federal Independence Party in Kenya; or by securing political equality in a multi-racial government, e.g. the R.D.A. in French tropical Africa. (c) *The political party*, which competes with other parties in periodical elections, accepting the constitutional *status quo* in order to do so, e.g. the C.P.P. to-day, the Sierra Leone People's Party, or the B.D.S. in Senegal. (See J. S. Coleman 'The emergence of African political parties'; essay in *Africa Today*, pp. 226–7.)

There are obviously grave difficulties confronting any African Christian who considers whether he can play a part as a member of any political party. Some of these will be noticed in a later chapter. The greatest obstacle of all is the bitterness involved in the political struggle. Movements and associations which, unlike genuine parliamentary parties, are not liable to find themselves bearing the burden of government, are naturally much more irresponsible in their demands and claims. Moreover the lack, in the original form of Crown Colony government, of anything resembling 'Her Majesty's most loyal Opposition', tends to make all opposition appear disloyal and subversive, and so aggravates the bitterness and secrecy in the nationalist movements.

Yet, in spite of the evident danger, these things constitute a challenge to African Christians to make their contribution within the various organizations. There are some extremist groups with which Christians will find it impossible to identify themselves. But the idea that members of the Church may only subscribe to the most 'moderate' political opinions is dangerously untrue. At all periods of history there have been great 'left-wing' and revolutionary Christians, as well as cautious and conservative Christians. As far as possible the ambassadors of Christ should be found in all political groups, bringing a deeper spirit of toleration by the very fact of recognizing as brethren Christians in other parties than their own.

Christian leaders from East Asia meeting at Bangkok in 1949 emphasized this inescapable responsibility of the Church in those countries that are moving into new political freedom. They recognized the fact that democratic institutions and values, divorced from their original Christian motive, exist in a moral and religious vacuum and tend to break down; and they urged: 'The Christian has the task of redefining and reinforcing these institutions and values in the light of the Christian faith, supplying a moral dynamic which they lack to-day.'[1]

The same idea was finely expressed by Professor K. A. Busia, when he wrote:

1. *The Christian Prospect in Eastern Asia*, p. 116.

82

Differences of Opinion

The creation of the welfare state means the assumption of wider activities and powers by those who govern. The opportunities for public dishonesty correspondingly increase. The democratic society cannot be built unless dishonesty and corruption are overcome or at least effectively curbed. The test for the Gold Coast and Nigeria in this sphere will prove more severe than learning to work the constitutional machinery and acquire the technological competence necessary for building a democratic welfare state. Our hope is that we will pass the test and be able to take our places as respected members of the community of nations, and make our contribution towards the peace of the world and the enrichment of human life.[1]

To the achievement of that high ideal Christians have a unique contribution to offer – but they must make it from the inside.

1. 'The Gold Coast and Nigeria on the road to self-government; essay in *Africa Today*, p. 300.

CHAPTER SIX

Racialism and Nationalism

RACE relations in Africa and the growth of African national-ism are subjects on which a great many books have been written. One chapter is obviously inadequate for topics of such burning importance and such complexity; yet a book on Christianity and politics in Africa which never faced these issues would be but a cowardly and ineffectual beating about the bush. For it is on these points more than anywhere else that Christians in Africa, of whatever race, need to know whether their faith can throw any light or set up any stan-dards of judgement.

Those who write on race and nationalism in Africa from a Christian standpoint tend to be either propagandist or ponti-fical. There are the warm-hearted Christian commentators and journalists – and thank God for them! – who burn with indignation at injustice and hypocrisy, and whose books, punctuated with examples of the worst manifestations of colonialism and white supremacy, are designed to expose certain evils and win sympathy for certain causes. On the other hand, there are some writers who have carefully examined the Biblical teaching on race and nationalism, have weighed the evidence of anthropology, and economics, and enumerated the historic motives which brought about the present *status quo*, in order to provide the student with the facts from which to assess the problems. This chapter, while it cannot make a comprehensive appraisal of all the factors, is an attempt to give to Christians of all races, who are at this moment having to make decisions in the midst of the African situation, some guidance in answer to the ques-tions: 'What should I think about this as a Christian, and what should I be doing?'

The tension in Africa is terribly intensified by the combina-tion and interaction of two factors, namely, race-discrimination and the political control of Africans by foreigners. (The necessary modification of this phrase in the case of the 'plural' societies will be considered later.) In some parts of the world these problems have occurred singly. The United States, for example, completed her struggle for political independence before she had to face the evils of racialism in her midst; neither problem was much complicated by the other. But in Africa the racial and the political issues are everywhere intertwined, and each aggravates and inflames the other. We shall try to deal here with each one separately because that undoubtedly helps us to *think* more clearly: but we must remember that when we have to *act* in the midst of the situation the two problems will not in fact be separate, and our decisions must take both into account. However much the theorists would like to do so, we cannot solve these problems one by one.

RACE

One of the puzzling facts which the Christian cannot ignore is that the idea of a chosen people lies at the heart of the Old Testament. The supreme act of God on which Israel's whole faith was built up was the deliverance from Egypt, by which He called a collection of clans and formed them into His own peculiar people who by custom, country, and culture were to remain separate from other tribes, and through whom God's blessing was to be mediated to the whole world. The tragedy of Israel was that, having learned by slow and painful discipline to keep herself untainted from the surrounding paganisms, she turned her purity into mere exclusiveness and refused to fulfil her mission to the world. She thought that God had chosen her for her own sake rather than for the sake of mankind; she did not want to believe that God could care for the other nations.

It is extraordinary to see what a strange power that Old Testament story has over the minds of men. Its broad outlines present a pattern to which the human experience of many peoples seems to correspond; it influences their thinking and their reactions; it becomes what the sociologists call a 'myth'. This happened to the Negro slaves in the American plantations. They saw themselves as the slaves of Pharaoh, 'way down in Egypt's land', and even those who knew they would never see their Moses in this world looked forward with longing to the Jordan of death and the Promised Land beyond.

It is an ironical trick of history that at the very time that Africans in a white man's country were living within that myth, other white men in Africa were doing exactly the same. Laurens Van der Post has revealed how the Afrikaaners have been dominated by the myth:

In the *Book* they found their inspiration and their comfort. They came out of Europe like the Israelites out of bondage in Egypt to search for their promised land. ... The particular myth of my countrymen presupposed just such a journey as the Great Trek through a great unknown wilderness to a land of promise.[1]

It is important that every Christian in Africa should understand this, and should learn also the interpretation of the Bible by which Christians of the Dutch Reformed Church justify their doctrine of race segregation. The original unity of the human race as created by God, they argue, was broken by sin; but God, for the purpose of restraining and mitigating the effects of disunity, introduced the divine order of separate nations and races. This difference of race is fixed and, like the establishment of human law and government, forms part of the natural order which Christians must respect. The original unity of all men can be restored by the abolition of all sin, but this can only be realized at the 'end of the world', and any attempt to anticipate that divine event is a rebellion against the natural order and a kind of anarchy. This imposes upon Christians the duty of taking action in society to keep the races apart.

With regard to the relationship of Christians belonging to different races, a variety of views are held within the Dutch Reformed Church. Some hold that unity in Christ is a

1. Laurens van der Post, *The Dark Eye in Africa* (Hogarth Press, 1955), p. 120.

'spiritual' unity only; it is not to be embodied in existing
Churches or social structures, but requires of all Christians
a concern for just treatment and right relationships among
races which are separated from one another. The Bloem-
fontein Conference of the Missions Council of the Dutch
Reformed Churches in South Africa in 1950, however, was
not satisfied with this view. It proclaimed that:

in spite of separation, the unity of the faith must, however imper-
fectly, be practised. . . . We may acknowledge that, especially for
practical reasons, it is without doubt more useful to organize
whites and non-whites separately. But that does not mean that we
have finished our task. We are members of the same body and need
each other. It is imperatively necessary that our Churches do not
merely ·confess unity in Christ as an article of our faith, but that
they also apply it in practice, for instance, in family devotion.

It is good to remember that leaders of the Dutch Reformed
Church have at least made such a statement. Nevertheless,
while we must always honour every sincere opinion, other
Christians cannot but take note of the falsity of their exposition of Scripture.

The Bible always recognizes that man has his existence in
a social context; his nationality, just like his family, is an
important element in his being, and the existence of separate
peoples has the divine affirmation. But the Biblical emphasis
is placed upon the common kinship and ancestry which
unites the various races; there is no evidence whatever of
any divine order of fixed difference and perpetual separation.
Different nations, regarded as political entities, have their
responsibility and destiny in God's purpose; but the world
of the Bible is always a very inter-racial and cosmopolitan
society, with Hittites at home in the neighbourhood of
Jerusalem, a Jewish woman marrying a Persian King, and a
North African carrying the Cross of Christ. And the question
of 'colour' simply never arises. Indeed, colour-consciousness
as we know it was never thought of before the seventeenth
century, when Europe first began to extend its empires over
the rest of the world.

It is true, of course, that the Jews were commanded to

87

keep themselves racially separate from other peoples. But there was only one chosen race; the whole point about Israel was that they, and their separatism, were unique. Nowhere is it suggested that every race is under the same obligation to keep itself apart.

The supreme fallacy in that interpretation of the Bible is that it ignores the New Testament. We might indeed say that the one social phenomenon with which the first Christians openly came to grips was the racialism of the Jews. At the beginning of his ministry, Jesus Himself flung the challenge with his provocative words in the synagogue at Nazareth (Luke 4. 24–30).[1] Pentecost was an inter-racial occasion, and the first obvious contention in the Church arose over the question of discrimination between Christians of Jewish birth and those from other races (Acts 11. 1–18). The issue raised by Peter's encounter with Cornelius came to a head after the mission to Galatia, and Paul was the champion of the inclusive, non-racial conception of the Church which was officially accepted at the Council of Jerusalem (Acts 15).

'No distinction' was one of the catch-words of the Apostolic age (Acts 11. 12; 15. 9; Romans 3. 22, 10. 12). The Chosen People on the grounds of race has been superseded by the new Israel on the grounds of faith; the call to be separate applies henceforth only to the Church's relationship with the 'world'. If indeed racial segregation had ever been a divine order introduced to mitigate the disunity wrought by sin, it clearly must belong to the same category of protective law as that which permitted and regulated divorce.

With regard to divorce, Christ admitted that under the old dispensation it had been written 'for your hardness of heart'; but in the new, free dispensation inaugurated by Christ, man's terms of reference are no longer bounded by human failure but are carried back to the original, unmarred purpose of God, 'from the beginning of the creation' (Mark 10. 4–9). So also with regard to race, the only 'natural law'

1. This revolutionary attitude is maintained throughout the ministry; see John 4. 9; Luke 11. 30–2; 13. 28, 29.

to which the Christian has the right to refer is that which derives from the original unity of God's creation: 'he made of one every nation of men for to dwell on all the face of the earth.' (Acts 17. 26).

We may respect the integrity of Christians who differ from us and recognize that we are still members one of another; but nevertheless if we see them turning back from the new dispensation of the Gospel to any older human bondage we are compelled to resist them 'to the face', because they stand condemned, just as Paul withstood Peter on exactly the same sort of issue because he saw 'that they walked not uprightly according to the truth of the gospel' (Galations 2. 11–14). Undoubtedly we can say of the defence of segregation from the Bible, as Albert Barnes said a century ago of the similar defence of slavery, that it 'is to be and will be abandoned and men will wonder that any defence of such a system could have been attempted from the Word of God.'

But in fact what we are dealing with in Africa is not the mistaken theology of a minority of sincere Christians, but the scornful prejudice, the cold refusal to treat other human beings as persons, the denial of dignity and worth, the utterly inexcusable injustice and the flagrant self-interest which so many white people far beyond the borders of South Africa exhibit in their thinking and their treatment of all non-whites. And this in turn may lead to a burning racial hatred in Africans themselves.

No Christian teaching, however mistaken, has ever attempted to justify such attitudes. They are evils which many Christians, perhaps, may need to repent of, and which all must fight. To compromise with the evil, to postpone the fight, to hope for some gradual improvement which will exempt us from the scandal and the pain of an immediate and absolute stand in this matter, is to deny Christ in Africa.

The practical stages by which colour bars and discrimination are to be removed will differ in various territories, and Christians may not always agree as to the best procedure of reform. But above all, we should strive to maintain co-operation and patience in the Church as a whole as it engages in this struggle. It will make a great difference to the health of the Body of Christ in Africa if Christians of all races can be fellow-combatants in this fight. It is important, too, to hold together, as far as possible, the very active pressure groups and the less active main body of the Christian community. This can only be done if the Church as a whole wakes up to the revolutionary nature of its calling. And that revolution demands both passion and patience.

To do any good in South Africa one would have to be very patient with Europeans. *They* are the Problem Children who most need patience, and there are European people like Olive Warner whose service to Africans consists partly in having patience with other Europeans. This patience has nothing to do with apathy – it is something cultivated only by people who care a great deal.[1]

AFRICAN NATIONALISM

Should Christians of any race play an active part in what we can describe generally as the nationalist movement? It has already been suggested in earlier chapters that they should, but it is important that all should understand their *Christian* grounds for doing so.

We must honestly recognize that the Bible as a whole does not lend support to the idea that every people has its own 'national home', which is divinely ordained for it, and to which it has exclusive rights of possession. It appears that the living God accepts and works through the hard facts of history, and history consists very largely of the movements of peoples and the rise and fall of empires. Israel believed that she was divinely commissioned to invade and occupy the territory which had for about five hundred years belonged to the 'Canaanites and Amorites'. Christ Himself steadily refused to be drawn into the nationalist movement of his day; and when the Apostles commanded Christians to be subject to every ordinance of man, they were writing to members of subject races under foreign colonial government.

Once again we see that if we look to the Bible for some

1. Reginald Reynolds, *Beware of Africans* (Jarrolds, 1955), pp. 294–5.

unchanging principle we shall be disappointed. We shall not find support for any tidy slogan such as 'Africa for the Africans', nor for any simple condemnation of colonialism as such. Christians in Africa will not find the Bible doing their thinking for them. What they will find in it is a growing understanding of God's nature and His purpose for all men. Armed with that insight they must stand in the midst of the tensions of Africa, and hear the call of God coming to them out of that situation, and give their responsible and contemporary answer in obedience to Him.

In order to think clearly about the African urge towards independence we must look first for a moment at the vexed subject of colonial power. It is extraordinarily difficult for us to-day to enter into the mind of a previous generation, but there is not the slightest doubt that the great missionaries of the mid-nineteenth century had a profound conviction that colonial empire and Christianity were fully compatible. In the letters of David Livingstone and Alexander Mackay appears an unquestioning assumption that the Gospel and Western civilization were a double gift tied up by God in one parcel. The white man's burden was a burden of guilt, the sense of a debt to be repaid; it is this which has inspired Albert Schweitzer to offer his life at Lambaréné, and also inspired Christians to colonize in order to civilize. It was Christian reformers who several times tried to persuade the British Government to found a colony at Mombasa in order to combat the Zanzibar slave trade, and several times they were refused. It was largely due to the effective public meetings addressed by Bishop Tucker that a reluctant British Parliament agreed to extend a Protectorate over Uganda. It is too easy to be cynical to-day about motives which we no longer share, but unless we recognize that they were sincerely and passionately at work in the missionary founders of many of the younger Churches we shall fail to understand those Churches in our own time.

For many of the Chiefs who first embraced Christianity and most of the first African ministers and Church elders accepted just as naïvely this innocent and optimistic conception of the role of the white man in Africa. In some, at least, of the African Churches that first generation of leaders is still alive; and in any case, because of its conservative tendency the Church is slow to abandon that old idea in spite of so many factors which prove it untrue to-day. Missionaries also have too often been guilty, not of deliberately perpetuating the old conception, but of failing to give the matter any serious thought at all until it is too late.

The old 'argument of Empire' is still alive to-day, and no honest person can deny that the evidence quoted is, as far as it goes, incontrovertible. Europe has the capital, the technological and scientific skills, and the wealth of experience which Africa still needs. When every possible criticism has been made of the policies or conduct of colonial government and European settlers, it remains true that in most parts of tropical Africa the over-rule of the colonial powers has brought Africans along the road of well-being, as perhaps nothing else could have done. The interest of some of the European powers in African political advancement must be accepted as genuine, however frustrating may be the slowness of the programme or the total lack of any timetable at all. The fear of 'handing over the people' to an opportunist minority is at least an honest scruple, however much it may be over-worked as an argument. The idea that the historically privileged nations have a God-given responsibility towards the undeveloped peoples is one which the Bible certainly appears to support.

And yet, to-day, the exercise of colonial rule by one people over another must appear to us very differently, not because we are more Christian than an earlier generation but because history, as it were, has switched on a new set of lights.

In the first place many Europeans as well as Africans have experienced a good deal of disillusionment. We have grown realistic enough to know that it was not only Christian idealists who went out to colonize the backward peoples. There was exploitation, aggression, trickery, and scorn, as well as service and sound government. We realize that the much advertised schemes of economic expansion, which do

indeed raise the standards of life in many lands, do so inci-
dentally, but would certainly never had been launched had
that, rather than the advantage of the initiators, been the
primary motive. We know also that very often service, like
capital, is only given on the giver's terms; the fallacy that
technical and administrative assistance cannot be given
without foreign control seems to be generally held.

Besides, we are at last waking up to the fact that in the
modern world – the post-war, post-revolutionary world –
it is no longer tolerable to maintain towards any people that
attitude which is inherent in the colonial relationship.
Paternal trusteeship is a splendid ideal where it is exercised
with the consent of a people who are mainly passive or lack
competent representatives of their own. It is quite another
thing in changed circumstances, when the subject peoples
are distrustful of the way they are being led, and no longer
acquiescent in their dependent status. An astonishing feature
of the present time is the naïve materialism of so many
Europeans, who are incapable of understanding that
Africans may care more passionately for intangible gains
such as freedom and responsibility than for a higher standard
of living. They share the bewilderment of the Governor
General in Java, at the time when the Dutch leaders there
realized that their Empire was tumbling about them. 'I cannot understand it,' he complained to Laurens van der Post;

Look what we have done for them. Look at the schools and the
hospitals we have given them. A hundred years ago the population
was only a few million, to-day it is nearly sixty million. We have
done away with malaria, plague and dysentery and given them a
prosperous balanced economy. Everyone has enough to eat. We
have given them an honest and efficient administration and
abolished civil war and piracy. Look at the roads, the railways,
the industries – and yet they want us to go. Can you tell me why
they want us to go?

And Van der Post felt compelled to reply: 'Yes, I think I can:
I'm afraid it is because you've never had the right look in the
eye when you spoke to them.'[1]

1. Van der Post, *op. cit.*, pp. 90–91.

But nationalism is not simply the result of bad race relations, the wrong look in the eye. It is an inevitable psychological reaction to colonial over-rule, and it is a chain reaction which leaves none of the subject peoples unaffected. Dr Hendrik Kraemar calls nationalism 'the illegitimate child of colonialism'. The presence of that child alters the whole situation.

There is yet a further truth which Christians are coming to recognize in this matter, one which is indeed inherent in their understanding of man's nature – namely that colonial power, however idealistic, is essentially one of those things which go bad. All arbitrary power over other people is corrupting and destructive, inevitably creating the inter-actions of paternalism with servility, domination with frustration, pride with an inferiority complex. The sooner any colonial rule is ended the less will its initial good effects be damaged by the bad relations which inevitably follow.

The same realism ought to characterize the Christian's attitude towards nationalism, for here, as in colonial rule, we must recognize both the ideal and the demonic elements latent in it. Subject peoples wait for the day when they will become the masters of their own destiny and the builders of their own responsible society. That surely is a necessary part of that full-grown humanity which the Church in the name of the Son of Man must demand for all men.[1]

1. For this reason, perhaps, Christians concerned with constitutional patterns should give more than a passing thought to the advantages of an indirect electoral system. The politicans whose technique consists mainly in swaying a mass vote are always in favour of a common, one-level system of election. But Gandhi in India, and many Christian thinkers elsewhere, have preferred a scheme whereby every village or sub-district should elect one of their own people to sit on a sort of district electoral college, and so on by a system of indirect election up to the central government. In this way even the humbler members of the community, who know whom they can trust in their own village though they can never understand the issues before a huge constituency, will be given that measure of real responsibility which they must exercise in order to avoid being either individual pawns or a proletarian mob. But of course countries which have already organized their own direct elections are not likely to undertake such a major change of constitutional pattern.

The objections raised against the claims for self-deter-
mination are generally of three kinds, political, cultural, and
economic. The *political* argument is some variant on the
theme: Are they ready for self-government yet? But, strangely
enough, the question is almost irrelevant. Almost all honest
African leaders will say that they do not feel ready for complete political responsibility. But no one can learn to drive a
car until the instructor takes his hands off the controls; and
if the police insisted on a hundred per cent road safety there
would be no cars on the road at all. Besides, a glance at the
political scene in Africa to-day will reveal that in fact there
is no logical ratio between the degree of African independence in various countries and the political competence of the
African inhabitants.

The *cultural* objection lays stress on the need to guarantee
the preservation of the values of western civilization. Those
who argue on these lines point to the rather third-rate,
recidivist way of life which can be found in some of the
smaller non-European countries which now enjoy independence. In reply to this the Christian, whatever his race, must
dare to affirm that God is not interested in the survival of
Western civilization as such. It only has value inasmuch as
it expresses certain ideals and standards of thought and life
which are of eternal worth. Any attempt to secure, for
example, 'the British way of life', by a denial of the things
which alone give that much abused phrase any value –
respect for human personality, for liberty, for tolerance –
would end in destroying what it sought to perpetuate.

The *economic* argument takes two forms, stressing either
the needs of the African territories for European skill and
capital to develop their resources, or the economic weakness
and waste of small self-contained territories in the modern
world. With regard to the first of these, Christians are called
to witness in the world to the fact that service and assistance
can be given without domination: 'and they that have
authority over them are called Benefactors. But ye shall not
be so: but he that is the greatest among you, let him become as the younger; and he that is chief, as he that doth

serve' (Luke 22. 25–26). As Reginald Reynolds has said:

Unless their concern for 'Backward Countries' is all hypocrisy they can give even better service – with a better chance of success– to a free country. There are obvious reasons for that. You can work *with* people, instead of always coming up against sullen or open hostility.[1]

If, however, it is pointed out that in this world no one is going to invest capital or provide administrative and technical assistance except on a hard bargaining basis, then we must surely insist that Africans themselves should be free to strike what bargain they can. As long as Africans feel that the key to the front door is in European hands, they regard with deep misgiving every new economic development in their territory; but let them only get the key firmly into their own hands, and at once they throw wide the door to foreign capital and personnel. In East Africa, where Africans have no effective control of economic policies, they are pathologically suspicious of all development. But in West Africa, wherever Africans have the control of immigration and development, they are eager to attract European and American enterprise. Then follows the discovery, which otherwise they cannot make, that only by achieving real national stability can they continue to draw to their country the foreign capital on which so much depends. In a brilliantly realistic essay on African development, in which he fully recognizes that Europe and Africa may be mutually inter-dependent and complementary to one another economically, the Secretary General to the Commission for Technical Co-operation in Africa South of the Sahara has written:

Even if the Africans are not ready to participate fully, on terms of equality, in the type of modern economic activities which require efficiency and knowledge, they must be given an equal chance or, better still, they must be put, thanks to their political advances, in such a position that they can formulate their own terms for European enterprise taking place in their territories: taxation;

1. Reynolds, *op. cit.*, p. 79.

nationality; rules of employment; wages; etc. [We should include immigration control as a priority.] . . . Whatever association there should be between an Africa composed of self-governing units applying their own economic criteria, on the one hand, and Western Europe and the West in general, on the other, should be the result of bargaining on equal terms and on the basis of mutual economic interests.[1]

The second line of argument is concerned with the economic necessity for big units of political and economic control, larger than any of the territories which might conceivably become self-governing African states. If the economists are unanimously on the side of the big battalions it is not for the Christian, as such, to argue with them. What the Church is bound to say, however, is that it is desperately important that any policies prepared for Africa should take into account other factors in the life of man besides the economic ones.

It does seem, then, that obedience to the call of God, as it comes through the living context of the present situation in Africa, demands that Christians of all races should actively engage, as opportunities present themselves, in the effort to bring to an end as early as possible the subordinate and dependent political status of African people. This obligation does not arise from any fixed principle of inalienable rights, but from the recognition that failure to do so in the present circumstances is to frustrate inexcusably the achievement by some human beings of their full potential stature and dignity, as responsible citizens making their own contribution to the common wealth of mankind and the service of God.

Yet, as has already been said, Christians, of all men, are bound to discern the demonic as well as the ideal features of nationalism. When men are kept waiting for self-realization they begin to struggle for it. Struggle inevitably narrows sympathy; frustration breeds bitterness; an over-riding cause makes the end justify any means; nationalism, as has

1. Paul Henry, 'The European heritage: approaches to African development'; essay in *Africa Today*, p. 126.

been horribly demonstrated in Europe, so easily becomes a volcano-movement of human passions which sweeps men into a tide of emotion in which conscience and private judgement are drowned. This need not happen, perhaps, but the man or the group which seeks to call up the spirit of nationalism must beware lest that spirit swells into a demon with a very ugly face that will corrupt all that is good and legitimate in the movement. The Christian Church in Africa must on no account espouse the cause of nationalism in order to curry favour and win the support of the masses. Every Christian has certain loyalties to his Master, and to his Master's methods, which must over-ride all other claims and prohibit his participation in *some* of the nationalist organizations. The Church is called to a ministry of reconciliation and cannot take up the weapons of hatred, lying, and terror.

Nevertheless we cannot lightly dismiss the dilemma which confronts the ministers of the Church in some parts of Africa when members of their flock ask them whether, if frustration and despair reached breaking point, it would be legitimate for them to join in a rising or a war of liberation. Honest men who have often heard extolled the glories of the great Christian liberators of the past – William the Silent, Gustavus Adolphus, William Tell, George Washington, Garibaldi, and others – cannot give a slick, dogmatic answer. We feel that in face of the appalling wastage of human life and the seeds of bitterness that are sown, the use of force must at all costs be avoided. Yet if passivism is right for one continent it must be right for all.

Much depends on whether the white Christians in Africa will be bold enough to make common cause with Africans in their efforts to achieve responsible citizenship by strongly radical, but legitimate means. They must not fail to warn their African fellow-members in the Church of the dangers of a flood tide of emotion and of the need to think clearly of the values that are at stake. But they can only dare to give that warning if they themselves are ready to stand under the judgement of the Word of God, and to see the corruption at the heart of colonial power just as clearly as they see the sleeping demon in nationalism. Where they have freedom to act, white Christians should openly do everything in their power to bring to a rapid end the dependent status of the African people. If this involves conflict and misunderstanding, they should not seek a greater detachment from the issues than their African fellow-Christians can enjoy.

Nor should we ever forget to pray in deepest sympathy with those leaders of the Church and of the Missions in some areas who have to decide a terrible question: whether it is better to remain silent in order to stay and sustain the Church's work and even its very existence, or to speak out and be removed rather than compromise Christ's Gospel with an acquiescence that He Himself would not own. Their dilemma is most painful; we can only pray and never judge.

THE MULTI-RACIAL SOCIETIES

As Christians we must always try to be responsible in our thinking, and this means that we must not simplify the issues. There is no obvious Christian answer to the problems of Kenya, where more than one nationalism is at work, nor to the different problems of the Central African Federation, of French Senegal (with a white population equal to that of Kenya), and of the Union of South Africa. The factor which puts these territories into a separate category is the climate, which has made it possible for Europeans to settle as permanent residents and to bring up their children as 'natives' of the country. The ratio of the white to the black population is therefore much greater than elsewhere; but even so, this does not mean that they are a very high percentage. In Southern Rhodesia there are about 27 Africans to every white person, and in Northern Rhodesia there are 41. In Kenya there are 131 Africans to every white, in Tanganyika 350 and in Nyasaland about 600. Even in the Union the white population is only about one-fifth of the total. Yet some of the whites in East and Central Africa, as well as the great majority in South Africa, believe in permanent white supremacy for these territories.

On the other hand a great many Africans are thinking in terms of eventual African self-government for these areas, for the idea of 'partnership' seems to them unreal and sophisticated, and fails to satisfy the aspirations of the politically conscious among them. The great majority of the African population is at present illiterate, and those who could act as responsible leaders in the community are much fewer than the white people who can do so. But that will not always be so. And, unless there is a deliberate denial of opportunity to Africans, the time is bound to come when those of them who can bear the highest civic responsibility will out-number the non-African population.

The Church must not ignore the very grave dangers latent in the situation. The two 'nationalisms' at present operative on opposite sides of the issue are bound to lead to calamity. If, however, we have rightly interpreted the demands of God within the situation of Africa to-day, then we can say that the Christian faith indicates a clear and creative, albeit a difficult, way through. We have already seen that, as Christians, we can find no justification for white dominance, nor, on the other hand, for an unthinking 'Africa for the Africans' policy. We believe that the Biblical understanding of God's purpose in the present situation lays on us the obligation to end the subordinate, dependent status of Africans, as Africans, in any part of the continent, and to offer to all the opportunity of playing their full part in deter-mining their destiny and building, with all fellow citizens, their own responsible society. This demands the establish-ment of common citizenship in a multi-racial state in which, as more and more Africans are brought to mature responsi-bility, they will, numerically, take the greater share in determining policy. Eventually, if inter-racial strife can be replaced by mutual trust and common concern, political opinion will be determined by other interests than the bare consideration of race.

While it is not the purpose of this book to canvass Christian backing for one particular party or policy – indeed we have already seen that we must expect to find, and to respect, differences of opinion among Christians with regard to the practice and techniques of politics – we should be quick to recognize and support any political party or society which attempts sincerely to work out and apply in detail these conceptions of personal responsibility and citizenship which have been outlined above. The Capricorn Africa Society, for example, is making such an attempt in the multi-racial areas. The acid test, of course, of any political organization is not to be found in the intentions of its founders but in the practical proposals which its members are prepared to implement. This does not mean that Christians must always stand critically aloof from any political venture until they have a guarantee that all its good intentions will be certainly fulfilled. By committing themselves in some degree, in the early stages, Christians may help to ensure that the eventual practice of the white members does not fall short of the professed ideal, and that African nationalism or patriotism becomes something more than the sentiment of a single African race united in bondage against a common enemy.

The only natural soil for the flowering of patriotism, however, is the sentiment surrounding birth and childhood, family friendship, common language, a storehouse of songs and stories, the raw materials of a culture. Patriotism that is deep and sane, not demonic and enflamed, grows quietly from the roots of home and community.

There is cause for deep reflection, therefore, on the possibility of a federal pattern of development[1] within certain African territories, such as Uganda, where the different standards of development among the various tribes constitute the heart of the political problem. Some Africans there believe that the main tribal regions should develop into partly autonomous states within the framework of an overall Uganda federation. The colonial government, however, comes down quite firmly on the side of a unitary state. The

1. What is referred to here is a federated form of constitution within one territory, and is not to be confused with the federation of several existing countries, as was done in the Central African territories. That is an entirely different question.

Gold Coast, established as another unitary state, has seen the government strongly challenged by a party with a federal programme. The Wachagga and the Wasukuma, two of the most progressive communities in East Africa, are themselves federated organizations.

It is one thing to argue on economic grounds, as the Dow Report[1] does, that tribalism as a system of land tenure is inadequate and destructive, and even to recognize that, once land tenure is changed, tribalism as a social structure must collapse. It is quite another thing to ignore tribal loyalty as a spent force and to disregard completely these small local groupings in the pattern of the future. If, economically, the large bloc is necessary, some means must be found of creating such blocs out of the given material of the small local units in which real vitality and loyalty subsists. British colonial policy, by its use of Indirect Rule, has succeeded to some extent in keeping alive this local structure of society; but it has incurred the strong suspicion that it is 'dividing in order to rule', because it has seldom provided meaningful constitutional links between the legislative bodies of the African administration in the different regions, and the central legislature. As Margery Perham has said, tribalism should be sublimated rather than superseded.

This is, of course, only one aspect, the economic one, of the fundamental problem which confronts the multi-racial societies – the deep African rejection of complete Westernization. It is the gravest possible mistake for Europeans to suppose, because of the incredible technological success of modern Western civilization, that other cultures can offer no desirable alternative. Europe has learnt one way of looking at the world; Africa has another way. The white man must at least respect the African's right to be different, even if he is too slow to realize how much the world needs the African vision.

For example, the African sees man as a part of nature, who has to submit to nature's laws and live his life within the natural economy of his immediate environment; the Euro-

1. *Report of the East African Royal Commission* (H.M.S.O., 1955).

pean sees man as in control of nature, always attacking nature's intractability by a fresh application of scientific technology.

This explains why there is such a misunderstanding between Europeans and politically conscious Africans when they talk about economic progress. The Africans still accept the subsistence economy, taken as a total concept with all its implications, as the natural economy to which the European should somehow bring, as gifts, the most practical benefits of Western technology: the bicycle, easy transportation, sewing machines and the like. The Europeans consider what remains of the natural economy, after the impact of their own settlement and economic penetration, as a remnant of primitive barbarism from which, somehow, Africa should progressively and forcibly emerge.[1]

Or again, one European thinker of the post-war world has drawn attention to the new and changing conception of the meaning of human existence inherent in the modern Western assumption that 'one does not work to live, one lives to work'. This glorification of human effort and activity makes men value one another, not by what they are, but by the job they do, so that even the so-called brain-worker is 'harnessed to the social system and takes his place in the division of labour; he is allotted his place and his function among the workers; he is a functionary in the world of total work'. There seems to be no sphere of human existence that does not need to be justified by inclusion in a five-year plan and its technical organization.[2] This also is an aspect of Westernization which Africa profoundly rejects.

Such deep spiritual rejection of these and other aspects of modern Western culture, for all that Africa has been, and is still, fascinated by the white man's technical triumphs, is something that must be taken into account if we are to have the slightest hope of building together the emergent African peoples, with the Asian and European minorities, into one multi-racial community. For that community must be one

1. Paul Henry, *op. cit.*, p. 134.
2. See Josef Pieper, *Leisure the Basis of Culture* (Faber & Faber, 1952), pp. 43–5.

in which no group so dominates as to destroy the deep roots from which another group draws its spiritual vitality. For a long time this would mean a co-existence of cultures, but the ultimate pattern of the fully integrated society would be 'something new out of Africa'.

Humanly speaking, the task is so complex, and the pitch has already been so queered, that the chances of success are very slight. But the Church is called to a supernatural faith and hope, believing, as it has always done, that the grim 'either – or' of our man-made enmities can be redeemed by the creative 'neither – nor' of Jesus Christ, in whom is 'neither Jew nor Greek, neither slave nor free'. In that hope the Church is called to a ministry of reconciliation in the multi-racial territories; it must demonstrate first in its own life the depth of understanding and mutual enrichment which is possible when men 'come from the East and from the West and sit down together in the Kingdom of God'; and it must champion fearlessly the cause of equal opportunity for all to enter into the privileges and responsibilities of citizenship.

The fight against prejudice, bitterness, and self-interest will never be won in time, unless all men of goodwill in the Church forget their shibboleths and learn to accept one another as fellow combatants in the one Lord. 'Kenya,' said Bishop Beecher in 1954, 'must work out a plural society or perish within five years.' Yet Dr Oldham has written of the multi-racial areas with a sanguine optimism that every Christian must endorse:

It looks as though the fate of a continent were at stake. No one can say that an attempt to redeem the situation will succeed. Life never guarantees success to any human endeavour. What it offers us are new ways of thinking, living and acting that are good and rewarding in themselves, and the hope that, if we are loyal to them, our small lives may be granted some enduring historic meaning.[1]

1. J. H. Oldham, *New Hope in Africa* (Longmans, 1955), p. 96.

CHAPTER SEVEN

Political Action by Individual Christians

I T remains for us now to consider what individual Christians, or groups of Christians, may be able to do in the political field, over and above the witness which the Church as a whole can give through its official organs. There are varying degrees of political activity, and different Christians may feel called to play their part in different ways.

For all Christians, however, it is probably true to say that it is their duty to be as well informed as they are capable of being in the political and social affairs of their own region. This is not to say that every Christian has to be 'politically minded'. But in Africa at the present time, where there are so many strong emotions to grip quite simple people, and where there are so many unscrupulous and dishonest seekers after power to deceive and exploit the ignorant, all Christians have a very special responsibility to seek after as much understanding of the truth as they are able to achieve, even if it is only on a quite humble, local level. Every Christian school in Africa should take very seriously the periods in the curriculum devoted to civics and general knowledge, and Christians should press for the best possible use of literature and posters, which will spread widely a real awareness of what responsible citizenship means.

The Christian duty of being an informed member of society is especially important in a country where there is universal suffrage; but it is also vital in the developing African states, and indeed in all areas where government reflects public opinion in any degree at all. A Christian writer has put it this way:

We may feel that we ourselves have little opportunity for effective influence on such matters. The problems involved are often complex and experts disagree on them. But . . . it is public opinion which largely influences what the policies will be which the political parties will put forward at election time, and public opinion also greatly influences the decisions and choices which the Government makes on specific issues of policy during its period of office. It is true that for the detailed knowledge on which to make up our minds we must usually rely on the expert, but experts differ, and on the basis of their recommendations there is usually a choice between several alternative lines of practical policy. Public opinion is very influential in deciding which of these shall be chosen. We can all play our part in the formation of public opinion, for we all of us have some influence on those around us, and *the sounder and more informed we show our judgement to be the greater is likely to be our influence*. By taking the trouble to find out the facts and weigh up the judgements of others, as far as we have the opportunity, and by giving thought to the formation of our own opinions, we are therefore making a valuable contribution to a healthier and juster social order.[1]

One of the most effective contributions which some Christians may be called to make is organizing or participating in study groups concerned with the search for a Christian viewpoint and understanding of some of the outstanding problems confronting the politicians. The pooling of the experience of people of different backgrounds and different traditions of thinking, who share a common faith and concern, can lead to some very fruitful results. One of the best known of such bodies at the present time is the Christian Frontier Council. This is mainly a body of Christian laymen who endeavour to work out together, in a number of different groups devoted to various spheres of life, the bearing of Christianity on modern secular life. For example, after prolonged discussions held by university teachers and administrators with Christians in other professions, a series of pamphlets on the purpose underlying the universities was published; then a conference was convened at Cambridge in 1946; and, as a result of that Sir Walter Moberly was invited to write his profoundly influential book, *The Crisis in the University*. Somewhat similar proceedings in another group under the auspices of the Council led up to the pro-

1. John F. Sleeman, *Basic Economic Problems* (S.C.M. Press, 1953), pp. 174–5. The italics are mine.

duction of Daniel T. Jenkins' book, *The Doctor's Profession*. These books illustrate the tremendous importance of, and necessity for what Sir Walter Moberly has called 'lay theologians', who can work out the implications of the Christian faith in their own professional sphere of knowledge and action.

Turning now from the realm of thought and discussion to the realm of action – though the two are not really separate but overlapping – we must not ignore the field of local government as one in which African Christians have already for many years been playing a notable part. There is no need to stress this sphere of action, for in all parts of the continent Christians are making their contribution as Chiefs, as local administrators, and on district councils. We should be, perhaps, especially awake to the need for local government to develop more rapidly into a genuine constitutional component of the political structure of each territory. There is a real danger that under the special patronage of the colonial administrations the local Chiefs and their councils may exercise an authority which is too little challenged precisely because it lies outside the disciplines of a developing constitutional system. Professor Busia said in 1955:

The evolution of local government under the policy of indirect rule was too slow and not sufficiently sensitive to changes in the social structure resulting from trade and commerce and education. Thus, the Gold Coast, and to a lesser degree Nigeria, has reached the threshold of self-government without a firm foundation of local government.[1]

Christians must therefore always remember the importance of local government work, although that is only a part of their wider concern for justice and righteousness in the nation as a whole. To-day the real problems of Africa lie in the field of national politics and social organization, and Christian responsibility cannot be limited to the local levels only.

Another very important method of Christian action to which some may be called is the formation of what might be

1. Busia, *op. cit.*, p. 293.

called 'pressure groups'. This phrase may be used to describe two different things. There is one type of pressure group which represents nothing but the selfish interests and the hunger for power of a political faction or a commercial clique, which exerts its 'pressure' by means of propaganda playing upon the emotions of the people, and by private influence controlling the decisions of political leaders. But on the other hand there have been formed from time to time pressure groups of Christian thinkers and leaders, who in the most selfless way have devoted their time and energy, money and resources to advocate some special cause or to bring to pass some much needed reform.

One of the most famous of all such Christian groups was that which was known as the Clapham Sect. The most famous member of this brotherhood of Christian friends and warriors was William Wilberforce; but the elder statesmen of the group were Granville Sharp, the draper's apprentice who became a lawyer and fought many a legal battle for the rights of the underprivileged, and John Thornton, the businessman from Yorkshire who was uncle to Wilberforce, and in whose home at Clapham, near to London, the group held its regular meetings. The members of the brotherhood who lived at Clapham included also John Venn, who succeeded his father as vicar of the parish church; Charles Elliott, his brother-in-law; James Stephen, the Scottish lawyer and writer of pamphlets; Zachary Macaulay, who had once been an overseer on a slave-estate in the West Indies; Charles Grant, who became the most distinguished director of the East India Company; John Shore, who was later Governor-General of India; and Henry, son of old John Thornton. Other members of the group who had great influence were Thomas Clarkson, who first won over Wilberforce to the anti-slavery cause; the redoubtable Mrs Hannah More, friend of John Wesley and champion of Sunday Schools; Charles Simeon, the great evangelical preacher from Cambridge, and Thomas Gisborne, another outstanding preacher from Staffordshire; Thomas Babington, brother-in-law to Macaulay, and Josiah Pratt, first editor of the *Christian Observer* and, with John Venn and Elliott, one of the founders of the Church Missionary Society.

The manner in which this fighting band went to work has been well described by Dr Marshall Howse:

This group of Clapham friends gradually became knit together in an astonishing intimacy and solidarity. They planned and laboured like a committee that never was dissolved. At the Clapham mansions they congregated by common impulse in what they chose to call their 'Cabinet Councils' wherein they discussed the wrongs and injustices which were a reproach to their country, and the battles which would need to be fought to establish righteousness. And thereafter, in Parliament and out, they moved as one body, delegating to each man the work he could do best, that their common principles might be maintained and their common purpose be realized. In private intercourse they lived and acted almost as if they all belonged to an inner circle of one large family. They dwelt in one another's houses almost as a matter of course.[1]

Their most impressive and memorable victories were won in connexion with the abolition of slavery. But besides that they fought a long fight with the East India Company for the right of entry of Christian Missions to India, and they were instrumental in founding the Church Missionary Society and the British and Foreign Bible Society. They waged a prolonged warfare against duelling, drunkenness, lotteries, and cruel sports; and although they failed to judge truly the issue of the Corn Laws and the repression of the desperate working class, yet they achieved some measure of penal reform, they did a great deal to establish the first Factory Acts, and they fought the evil of the press gangs. They championed the cause of Roman Catholic and Free Church emancipation; and they were actively engaged in innumerable charitable concerns.

Where the Clapham Sect had been blind to the injustices of their society towards the working classes, another Christian pressure group arose forty years later to remedy this defect. These were the Christian Socialists, who gathered round Frederick Denison Maurice, the Chaplain of Lincoln's Inn

1. E. Marshall Howse, *Saints in Politics* (Allen & Unwin, 1952), p. 26.

and Professor at King's College, London. They included a group of law students from Lincoln's Inn, a couple of doctors, an architect, a chemist, a publisher, and several writers. Associated closely with them were one or two other clergy in other parts of the country.

They stood, a handful of men, midway between the 'haves' and the 'have-nots', claiming social justice for the underdog, but pleading that no mere political reform, only the Christian way of life, could make men free.[1]

The heart of all their activity was the weekly Bible reading which Maurice led in his house in Queen Square, London. But their study of the Word of the Lord brought them to take up the Sword of the Lord in a variety of most positive ways. At first they ran a night school for young hooligans from the London streets, and published a weekly paper called *Politics for the People*. Then they launched a number of trade co-operatives which, although they were not very successful in themselves, gave a great impetus to the spread of the co-operative movement throughout Britain; and they played a considerable part in getting through Parliament a bill which gave legal status to co-operative societies. They were soon faced with a problem which confronts, in one form or another, all such Christian 'pressure groups'; namely, the need to decide how far they could co-operate in social and political action with others who did not share their Christian faith. After a little hesitation Maurice decided that while the Christian Socialists must hold unshaken their conviction that only in Christ could men find liberation from the real source of all bondage, yet, as he put it, they should unite for practical purposes with all men of honest purpose, whatever their intellectual confessions, because they were now confronting the whole structure of their society in which 'competition is put forward as the law of the universe. That is a lie. The time has come for us to declare it is a lie by word and deed.'

So much space has been devoted to these two examples

1. Florence Higham, *Frederick Denison Maurice* (S.C.M., 1947), p. 59.

from past history because they illustrate all the problems and the potentialities of Christian pressure groups. It is their nature to deal with a limited number of concerns, and to fight for particular causes one by one. They are *not* political parties, and therefore cannot be expected to have a considered opinion and policy on every one of the affairs of state. But, because their interests are necessarily so narrowed down to particular fighting issues, all pressure groups have a peculiar temptation to intolerance and partisanship. Christians, if they form such groups, or participate in them, have therefore a special responsibility to guard against the subtle growth of untruth and biased thinking. It is very easy for pressure groups to become merely new vested interests standing in furious opposition to old ones. They tend to build up a bogey in the imagination, and talk about 'Them' as the undefined enemy who are responsible for every evil; to use the exaggerated jargon of an over-simplified and too-knowing judgement of the case – 'Of course *we* know what their promises are really worth'; 'It sounds all right but it's only propaganda to keep us quiet'. Christians ought not to be naturally more gullible than other men, but the state of mind which can take nothing at its face value, besides being extraordinarily tiresome, is certainly quite unchristian.

Both the Clapham Sect and the Christian Socialists made use of newspapers and political journalism as another field in which Christian individuals can make a most powerful contribution. Sometimes a letter sent to a newspaper editor, if it is published, may both influence and indicate public opinion and so contribute towards the pressure that is being brought to bear upon political leaders. A great many of the letters that appear in the press, however, are no more than a personal safety valve, or the product of people who enjoy exhibiting themselves in public; and because most readers realize this the letters do not carry any weight at all. In order to be effective, letters should be written only by individuals or groups whose opinion is valued either for their expert knowledge or for their influence in society. The best results are obtained when letters are carefully timed to form part of a series in a planned correspondence campaign, or combined with other forms of political action, such as a private approach to a minister by some official Church leader, or a question asked by some Christian member of the legislature.

In every part of Africa, where newspapers of an irresponsible kind spring up like mushrooms, there is the utmost need for Christian journalism and editorship. But it must be realized that this is highly skilled work, and unless it is undertaken by men with expert professional ability it will only discredit the Christian cause. Journalism is a sphere, moreover, in which it is particularly hard for the Christian to succeed. Good and pious opinions, with bits of local Church news, written with only amateur skill, can never compete with the products of professional journalism in commanding the attention of ordinary people. On the other hand, a Christian writer or editor cannot make use of the weapons of sensationalism, scurrility, and misrepresentation which often enable even the most poorly produced little newspapers to hold their place on the market. But just because this is such a difficult job it is all the more worth doing.

Good journalism demands sound judgement, broad tolerance, and courageous honesty, and these are gifts which the Christian Church should be able to offer. If there should be Christians who feel called to enter this field of action, they ought to be able to count on the caring and encouragement of the whole Body of Christ behind them. Above all, the Church must not countenance the idea that, just because the extremist newspapers are irreligious, Christian journalism must be cautious and reactionary. The characteristic of the Christian warrior, in politics as elsewhere, is not that he pulls his punches, but that he fights cleanly, and his enemy is not any particular group of men, but wickedness wherever it may be found. Africa badly needs newspapers that are strongly liberal and strongly Christian.[1]

1. There are at present a few illustrated monthlies published by Christian bodies in Africa, of which *Envol*, published in French at Léopold-ville by the *Société Littéraire d'Afrique*, and *The New Nation*, published in

Political Action by Individual Christians

Another field of activity which has a direct bearing on politics is the whole range of voluntary associations in trade and industry, including producers' and buyers' co-operatives, employers' associations and trade unions. Christians could participate more effectively in all such organizations, which provide large fields for social action and fellowship.

Undoubtedly the development of producers' co-operatives has in many different districts done more than any other factor to foster a sense of civic pride and loyalty, the growth of a 'modern' social structure, and a new faith in the future, which are the most reliable raw materials for the building of a responsible society. A striking instance of this is the Chagga confederation in the foothills of Mount Kilimanjaro. The success of this community is often attributed to the superiority of the Wachagga themselves; but, while no one would deny their outstanding qualities, it might just as well be argued in reverse that the co-operative structure which has been so carefully built up has fostered the development of the people to their fullest capacity, and might do the same to other people elsewhere. This is at least partly verified by the effect of the Bugishu Coffee Marketing Scheme in northeast Uganda, where a tribe which by all accounts was extremely backward has been brought forward into a progressive solidarity by the stimulus of a common enterprise.

English in Accra, maintain a very high standard of pictures and layout. *African Challenge*, published in English by the S.I.M. in Nigeria, is also good. These three, besides articles on religious and cultural topics, carry a limited amount of comment on general news. There is a great number of confessional and Mission journals all over Africa, but very few publish any general news or comment on secular affairs, and of these the Roman Catholic papers, such as *The African* in Rhodesia and Nyasaland, and *Munno* in Uganda, come nearest to being real newspapers competing with the secular press.

The greatest need is not for the production of more religious papers, but for Christian journalists who will launch secular newspapers in which the presentation of news and comment will be governed by a Christian ideal. There are a few such men, both African and European, whom it would be invidious to name here. They deserve more support and they need more concerted action.

It is unfortunate that in some African territories the colonial government has been too slow in welcoming and assisting the growth of co-operatives, with the result that a good many unrecognized associations had already come into being before official action was taken; these naturally regarded with suspicion the later overtures of government-sponsored organizations. This lack of confidence is, at least in British tropical Africa, largely unfounded, for the officers of the Cooperative and Labour Departments are by virtue of their training and their experience of the British labour movement, anything but government 'stooges'; and the services and advice they have to offer are not only urgently needed, but are likely to be more truly disinterested than those of a good many of the leaders of the unofficial associations. Christians have a very clear responsibility within the African co-operatives to encourage greater trust and full participation in the 'recognized' organizations.

Closely allied with the spread of co-operation is the development of trade unions. This is a new, but very significant growth in Africa. Since 1941, the British Colonial Office has been engaged in a drive to promote trade unions, and more than 1000 new unions have been established in the colonies. In Africa there are several factors which are opposed to the growth of unionism. The low level of industrialization and the high proportion of migratory labour result in a relatively small number of industrial workers who are in a position to organize themselves in a union. Tribal loyalties tend to break up the greater solidarity necessary for an effective association of workers. Africans with the necessary gifts of leadership have been drawn, on the whole, more into the direct struggle for political advancement than into the labour movement. In some areas governments have been definitely averse to the growth of unionism, and elsewhere the formation of African unions has been treacherously opposed by white unions – a disgraceful rejection of the true spirit of the labour movement in favour of the meanest form of organized selfishness. And yet, in spite of the difficulties and the unreadiness, there can be no field in which Christian influence is more urgently needed than the emergent trade unions of Africa.

There is a positive and a negative aspect of this need. On the positive side Christian leaders could help to give a 'soul' to the labour movement in Africa. In Britain both the Labour Party and the trade unions owed a great deal in their formative years to men of Christian faith; they instilled a passion for righteousness which saved the movement, at that time, from degenerating into mere self-interest. That contribution is not, at present, being made in the emergent trade unions in Africa; nor are they likely to catch any of that vision and that 'soul' through their link with the European labour movement in its present condition. The African unions of the future – and whatever appearances may now suggest, African unions are certainly going to wield an immense influence in another generation – will be without ideals unless Christians in Africa begin to implant them now.

On the negative side it can be asserted that unless Christians of all races strive both to win legal recognition of African unions and to establish in the unions the true desire for righteousness and integrity, the unions themselves will become the open door through which a great evil will enter and destroy. If the unions have to face official opposition, they will simply be driven underground, where they may seek in international communism the assistance and advice which they are denied elsewhere. And even where unions are officially encouraged, unless their leaders are committed to clear-cut moral standards and aware of the nature of the danger which threatens, the union will most certainly be used as the channel of communist infiltration in Africa, as elsewhere. Already this is beginning to happen. The Sudan Workers' Trade Union Federation, for example, one of the most significant union federations in the Arab world, already has strong Communist leanings. The rivalry between the Communist-dominated World Federation of Trade Unions, and the International Confederation of Free Trade Unions, has spread to many parts of Africa. In French Africa there are close links between the African trade unions and the French Communist Party. Repression is futile to deal with such a situation; what the unions need above all is strong, positive leadership by men who are not prepared to be dominated by any political party.

Finally, the fullest degree of Christian participation in politics is to join a political party, and to stand for member-ship of a legislative body. Enough has been said in this book already to make it plain that if a Christian feels truly called to play such a part in his nation's life, then he should go forward with this undertaking, believing humbly that he may indeed be the servant of Christ in such a sphere, and supported by the prayers of a Church which believes like-wise. The Church may sometimes feel that it could have made a more satisfactory choice of political leaders than the men who actually take up the task. In the same way many lay-men may feel they could have chosen more inspiring clergy; many parents may feel they could have chosen better teachers for their children. But in every professional field we must accept and deal with those to whom God has given the desire and the enthusiasm for the work, and not undermine them by a cynical distrust which Jesus Christ, who believed in even His weakest disciples, would never own.

This principle of making the best of the available material must be applied also to the Christian's support of one or other of the existing political parties. There are some parties, particularly in young and emergent societies, which are so extremist, or so opportunist, that Christians may feel it is impossible, for conscience' sake, to support them. But, for the rest, Christians should be ready to accept the human frailty that will be evident in every party and, without wait-ing for perfection, to give their support to whichever party, after due consideration, seems to them to approximate nearest to truth and justice. As we have already seen, they will not all choose alike.

Young Christians who are eager to carry their faith into the political field sometimes suppose that it should be possible to create a Christian party, commanding the support of the whole Church, and pursuing a policy that is worked out from Christian insight. It is conceivable that, in a situation where the only other parties were all blatantly materialist or dishonest, such a step might be necessary in order that Christians could conscientiously play any part in parliamentary government. But it is generally true that the formation of a Christian party has been advocated only by those Churches which hold that what is Christian opinion can be dogmatically laid down by Church authority, and that the Church has a divinely given responsibility to exercise temporal as well as spiritual power. There are such grave dangers in the formation of a Christian party that most Churches are strongly opposed to it. At its first assembly in Amsterdam, the World Council of Churches voiced this opposition in no uncertain terms:

The Church as such should not be identified with any political party, and it must not act as though it were itself a political party. In general the formation of such parties is hazardous because they easily confuse Christianity with the inherent compromises of politics. They may cut Christians off from other parties which need the leaven of Christianity, and they may consolidate all who do not share the political principles of the Christian party not only against that party, but against Christianity itself. Nevertheless, it may still be desirable in some situations for Christians to organize themselves into a political party for specific objectives, so long as they do not claim that it is the only possible expression of Christian loyalty in the situation.[1]

It is much to be preferred for Christians, each following his own intelligence and conscience, to be found in all parties, thus leavening the whole lump. The fact that members of the Christian Church, though divided by political adherence, nevertheless are united by a common faith, and sometimes fight together on the basis of that faith, is a greater witness to the significance of the Gospel than any single political philosophy could ever be. An example of this occurred in the British House of Commons during the 1920s, in the friendship and alliance between Sir Henry Slesser, a

1. *The First Assembly of the World Council of Churches*, ed. W. A. Visser t'Hooft (S.C.M., 1949), p. 81.

prominent member of the Labour Party, and Sir Robert Newman, the Conservative. On the common basis of religion and outlook, although then of different political parties, they became so united that they were known in the House as 'the Heavenly Twins'. Later Slesser wrote of his retirement:

Our little adventure to affirm our avowed Christian policy was over, yet some day, I pray and believe, someone will succeed where we, doubtless because of our deficiencies, failed. The alternative to Christian politics is Tyranny.[1]

It is a significant fact that in the young parliaments of the emergent African states Christians have early been called to high office. It would be invidious to mention particular men by name; but the Church may give thanks for them, and must not cease to pray for them. For of all professional tasks that of the political leader is perhaps most fraught with moral danger. The obvious temptations of corruption and graft may be resolutely cast aside because of their obvious nature. But there are other far subtler pitfalls. Christians will be facing at all times the fact that the political machine is so constructed, so geared to human nature, that it works best when such methods are employed as the Christian is bound to reject. The Christian politician must steadfastly refuse to make use of the mass hypnotism of propaganda, the smearing of political opponents, the exploitation of resentment and division, even though these are the methods which apparently get results.

Hardest of all is the slow, downward drag of living in a situation where it is taken for granted that a politician will act on assumptions which are completely contrary to Christian faith – the assumption that the driving power of human nature is personal greed, the assumption that human life is brutally competitive, the assumption that men can always be led by an appeal to their appetites. That is the moral atmosphere which has led some people to the conclusion that Christianity and politics do not mix. But a long line of Christian statesmen of many nations, who have lived heroic-

1. Sir Henry Slesser, *Judgment Reserved* (Hutchinson, 1941), p. 249.

ally through the slow martyrdom of being misjudged, and have stood steadfast amid the shifting tides of policy, give the lie to such a cowardly opinion. Africa, too, must add her own glorious names to the roll of 'saints in Caesar's household'.

CHAPTER EIGHT

Epilogue

AND what will be the end of it all? Will the Christian
Church, by participating responsibly in the field of politics,
eventually build the Kingdom of God on earth?

The question is worth asking; for the majority of politicians of the West have become so engrossed in means that
they no longer believe it is useful to consider the end.
Therefore the ideology of communism, with its positive
faith in the shape of things to come, is so much more dynamic. ·

The Christian also believes in the End. He has a conviction about it which colours all his thinking and shapes his
action. But he sees a pattern of history which is not the simple
thing of the communist's dialectic, but is so profoundly true
to life that it appears strange to men who look for an easy
slogan. In its world view, Christianity takes seriously both
tragedy and hope.

The Christian, whether he is pastor or politician or
humble man of God, recognizes the strange, catastrophic
element in human life. Sometimes it appears in the perverse
wickedness of individual men and women, sometimes as the
folly which seems doomed to blunder and slip just when
success is near. More often it is impossible to lay the blame
on any individual, for all alike are involved in the errors and
fears and unreliability of one another. We can partly understand why men are reacting in this or that way, but we are
powerless to prevent it. Great efforts of mind and heart and
will could find the solution of every one of Africa's problems,
and yet mankind, out of this tragic element in human nature,
might still turn away from the solution back towards disaster.
For across every page of the history of man might be written
the words, 'If only . . . ' By hard-won victories men gain
liberty, only to barter it for a mess of pottage. They wage the
painful war for righteous justice, only to find old tyranny

arising in a new guise. The Christian politician dare not treat any human society as an end in itself, nor believe that Utopia can be made by legislation and reform.

And yet, of all men, the Christian has the most profound hope. We shall not build the Kingdom of Heaven in this world; nevertheless God will give it to us. And all our planning and patience, our fighting and faithfulness, our longing and loss, will be related to the coming of His Kingdom, not as the builder's effort is related to the finished cathedral, but as the caterpillar's slow struggle for existence is related to the butterfly. Because we are the heirs of that Kingdom, and because the Kingdom is already within us, faith in the God and Father of our Lord Jesus Christ brings an absolute conviction that the end is in *His* hands, and an absolute demand to take the present moment into our own.

Because the Christian is confident about an end which is nothing but the gift of God, he is ready to take creative responsibility for the affairs of the world in which he lives. This is the secret of the profound optimism which Dietrich Bonhoeffer, the German pastor, described in the letters he wrote from his prison cell:

The essence of optimism is that it takes no account of the present, but it is a source of inspiration, of vitality and hope where others have resigned; it enables a man to hold his head high, to claim the future for himself and not to abandon it to his enemy. Of course there is a foolish, shifty kind of optimism which is rightly condemned. But the optimism which is will for the future should never be despised, even if it is proved wrong a hundred times. . . . Some men regard it as frivolous, and some Christians think it is irreligious to hope and prepare oneself for better things to come in this life. They believe in chaos, disorder and catastrophe. That, they think, is the meaning of present events, and in sheer resignation or pious escapism they surrender all responsibility for the preservation of life and for the generations yet unborn. To-morrow may be the day of judgement. If it is, we shall gladly give up working for a better future, but not before.[1]

The long fight for a righteous world will end in the divine

1. Bonhoeffer, *op. cit.*, pp. 25–6.

gift of the Kingdom of God, but no blow struck in that fight ever falls unnoticed. In the parable of Jesus the final word is: 'Come, . . . inherit the Kingdom prepared for you from the foundation of the world . . . Inasmuch as ye did it unto one of these my brethren . . . ye did it unto me' (Matthew 25. 34–40). So, like the House of Commons at the close of a long-fought session, the Church Militant will hear, as it were, the word of her release, 'Who goes home?'

Books for Further Reading

ANYONE who has read the foregoing chapters and wishes to study the subject more thoroughly will have to take into account two kinds of books: those dealing with Christianity and politics in general terms against a mainly European background; and those written about the social and political problems of modern Africa but without special reference to the Christian's responsibility. In his reading he will have to relate, as this book has attempted to do, the theory and theology of the first group of books to the particular situations described in the second.

There is, of course, a very wide range and a bewildering number of books emphasizing the responsibility of the Christian Church in the field of citizenship and politics, and explaining the Biblical and theological basis of it. Among the smaller books one of the first to be read should be *The Christian as Citizen*, by John C. Bennet, Professor of Theology and Ethics at the Union Theological Seminary, New York (United Society for Christian Literature, 1955). This is one of the outstanding new series of World Christian Books, which enlists experts to write for a world-wide public at a very low price. A somewhat different treatment of the same subject is M. B. Reckitt's *The Christian in Politics* (S.P.C.K., 1946), and, for those who like to read in French, an excellent small book is *L'Eglise, l'Etat, leurs relations*, by five contributors, Amblet, Kursner, Schadt, Vaney, and Wohnlich (Labor et Fides Press, Geneva, 1955).

Another small book which has had an influence out of all proportion to its size is *Christianity and World Order*, by G. K. A. Bell, the Bishop of Chichester (Penguin Books, 1940). This deals with Christian action in the sphere of national and international politics. Closely linked with it in intention is *Christianity and Social Order*, by William Temple, who was then Archbishop of York (S.C.M., 1942). This answers the question, 'Should the Church interfere?' and lays down the Christian principles regarding society and the State with great clarity. Another book by the same author is *Citizen and Churchman* (Eyre and Spottiswoode, 1941), which deals with the same question from the standpoint of the individual Christian, discussing his responsibility towards his country and his Church.

One other small book is worth attention because it is written particularly with the colonial territories and the younger Churches in mind. This is Max Warren's *Caesar the Beloved Enemy* (S.C.M., 1956). In these three lectures which he gave at the Virginia

Theological Seminary, U.S.A., Dr Warren tries to define the theological significance of imperialism and goes on to consider the responsibility of the Church in the modern Welfare State, especially as this emerges in the countries of Asia and Africa.

Among more advanced and comprehensive works on social and political ethics there are four which should claim the attention of serious students who are prepared for stiffer reading. The *Two Moralities*, by A. D. Lindsay (Eyre and Spottiswoode, 1940), discusses the tension between man's duty to God and to society. *Justice and Social Order*, by Emil Brunner (Lutterworth, 1945), develops a doctrine of the meaning of social justice from the teaching of the Old and New Testaments and of the Church. *The Free Society*, by John Middleton Murry (Dakers, 1948), like many others of his books, works out the implications for modern society of his conception of spiritual freedom. *The Realm of the Spirit and the Realm of Caesar*, by Nicholas Berdyaev (Gollancz, 1952), is a philosophical treatment of the concepts of Freedom, Authority, Community, Nationality, and so on.

A fifth important book on this subject is *The Social Teaching of the Christian Churches*, by Ernest Troeltsch, which is an historical approach to the question of Christian social responsibility. Written in 1911, it is still the classic textbook, tracing the development of Christian thought and influence on social reform and political change from the earliest times till the nineteenth century. The English translation by Olive Wyon was published in two volumes by Allen and Unwin in 1931.

Other historical works include Professor R. H. Tawney's *Religion and the Rise of Capitalism* (John Murray, 1926), which has had a very great influence on both theological and economic studies for the past thirty years. This has also been published in Penguin Books. It surveys the history of religious thought in Europe on social issues, particularly in the field of economics, from the late Middle Ages to the eighteenth century.

A much smaller historical work for the general reader is *The Church and the Social Order*, by S. L. Greenslade (S.C.M., 1948); this covers the period from the beginnings of the Christian era to the end of the nineteenth century, narrowing the field, as most of these books do, in the later chapters to the English scene only. The historical treatment is also followed in *The Christian Origins of Social Revolt* by W. D. Morris (Allen and Unwin, 1949), and in T. M. Parker's Bampton Lectures, *Christianity and the State in the Light of History* (Black, 1955).

Books for Further Reading

A more confined but important historical study is *Christian Socialism 1848–1854*, by Charles Raven (Macmillan, 1920), which examines the work of F. D. Maurice and his fellow founders of that movement; and a similar study, of an earlier Christian group, is *Saints in Politics*, by E. Marshall Howse (Allen and Unwin, 1952), which describes the personalities and activities of the 'Clapham Sect' (see pages 108–11 of this book). A recent work which throws a particularly interesting light on the problems of social and political responsibility in territories under colonial government is Dr Kenneth Ingham's *Reformers in India, 1793–1833* (C.U.P.,1956), which is an account of the efforts of early Christian missionaries on behalf of social reform.

One important aspect of the Church's responsibility in the political field is the Christian evaluation of Communism. A great number of books have been produced on this theme; one which succeeds in being most comprehensive in a small compass is *Communism and Christianity* by Father Martin D'Arcy (Penguin Books, 1956). Another valuable study has an almost identical title: *Christianity and Communism*, by John C. Bennett (S.C.M., 1949).

A certain number of other important books dealing with Christian political responsibility have been published in connexion with the ecumenical movement towards united thought and action among the Churches. The history of this movement has been described in another Penguin Book by the Bishop of Chichester, *The Kingship of Christ* (1954). There it will be seen that one of the major forces which have drawn and held the Churches together during nearly forty years has been the steady and concerted attempt to speak with a single voice in giving the Christian reply to the challenge of human social disorder. A huge body of material – studies, essays, reports, and surveys – testifies to the diligence with which the Churches have addressed themselves to this task. Here are some of the most important of the books that have been produced in this way:

The Church and its Function in Society, by W. A. Visser t'Hooft and J. H. Oldham (Allen and Unwin, 1937) was prepared as study material to be laid before the Oxford Conference of the Universal Christian Council for Life and Work.

The Churches Survey their Task (Allen and Unwin, 1937) is the report of the above conference.

The Church and the State is Volume VI of the full report of the Second Assembly of the International Missionary Council at Tambaram in 1938 (O.U.P., 1939).

Christianity and Politics in Africa

The First Assembly of the World Council of Churches (S.C.M., 1949) is the report of the assembly held at Amsterdam in 1948.

The Church's Witness to God's Design (S.C.M., 1948) was prepared by eleven contributors as study material for the Amsterdam conference. The chapter entitled 'The Gospel at Work in the World' provides much useful material on the work and witness of Christian Councils in regard to many social problems.

The Christian Prospect in Eastern Asia (New York, 1950) reports the findings of the first regional study conference of the Churches to be held in Asia, and is remarkable as the product of the joint thinking of a number of leading Asian Christians. *Christ – the Hope of Asia* (Madras, 1953) is the full report of a conference of the Study Department of the World Council of Churches at Lucknow in 1952.

Since the next assembly of the International Missionary Council is to meet in the Gold Coast at the end of 1957 – the first world conference of the ecumenical movement to be held on African soil – there should be a special interest in the study of the statements of these earlier conferences and in their application to the problems of Africa. A collection of extracts from most of the above books which deal particularly with Christianity and politics has been published by the World Council of Churches in a cyclostyled format called *Ecumenical Documents on Church and Society (1925–1953)* (Geneva, 1954), which should be a valuable tool for any student.

Turning now to books which deal specifically with the African situation we are confronted with a flood of recent writing of very varied quality. A most valuable general book is *Africa Today*, edited by C. G. Haines (O.U.P., 1955). This contains the addresses given at a conference of experts in many fields of African life which was convened in 1954 at the School of Advanced International Studies at Washington.

Another reliable and useful handbook is *Nationalism in Colonial Africa*, by Thomas Hodgkin (Muller, 1956). As a contrast to the rather stolid character of this work there are two exciting and provocative books written recently by non-Europeans. *Epitaph to Indirect Rule*, by Ntieyong U. Akpan (Cassell, 1956), is a Nigerian writer's study of English local government and his alternative suggestions for the emergent African societies; this should be read in conjunction with Ronald Wraith's *Local Government* (African Penguins, 1953). *Pan-Africanism or Communism?* (Dobson, 1956), by George Padmore, who is a Trinidadian, is a study of the political and economic structure of African rule in Africa, the alternative forms that it can take, and the means of establishing it.

Books for Further Reading

Two fascinating psychological studies which have provoked strong reactions are *The Dark Eye in Africa*, by Laurens Van der Post (Hogarth, 1955), which suggests profoundly the inner springs of racialism, and *Prospero and Caliban*, by O. Mannoni (Methuen, 1956), which explores the psychology of colonization as exemplified in Madagascar. This has much light to throw on the nature of white paternalism and the reactions of subject people. It also contains an important section on the function in Malagassy society of the *fokon'olona*, or village councils.

Finally there are those books which deal with the problems peculiar to a particular area of Africa, of which a few may be mentioned here. Anyone wishing to understand the racial policy of South Africa should read *Christian Principles in Multi-racial South Africa* (Johannesburg, 1954), which is the report of the Conference of Dutch Reformed Church leaders held in 1953 and is a statement of the convictions held by that Church. With it should be read the report of the Rosettenville Conference of the other main non-Roman Churches of the Union held in 1949, *The Christian Citizen in a Multi-racial Society* (Christian Council of South Africa, 1949). For a similar contrast, this time in individual terms, see Father Huddleston's *Naught for your Comfort* (Collins, 1956), and the reply *You are Wrong, Father Huddleston*, by Alexander Steward (Lane, 1956).

Race and Politics in Kenya (Faber, 1956) contains the correspondence between Elspeth Huxley and Margery Perham first published ten years ago, now brought up to date with an essay of reassessment by each of the joint authors. 'Adelphoi' is the pseudonym of a group of African and European Christians in Kenya who have written down the results of their prolonged discussion concerning the needs of that sorely divided territory, and their ideas for a Christian way ahead, in *His Kingdom in Kenya* (Hodder and Stoughton, 1953).

A bold Christian approach to the problems of the multi-racial areas of East Africa is to be found in J. H. Oldham's *New Hope in Africa* (Longmans, 1955). Dr Oldham writes as 'a loyal supporter' of the Capricorn Africa Society, but the book is by no means limited to an exposition of that society's aims and purposes, and contains much that is of universal application and of permanent significance for all who are concerned with the Christian approach to the needs and problems of Africa.